POTTERY

POTTERY

CREATING WITH CLAY

ROSEMARY ZORZA

DOUBLEDAY & COMPANY, INC.
GARDEN CITY, NEW YORK
1974

Frontis—Textured pottery planters by the author.
(Photo by Cynthia Brumback.)

Ceramic windbells by Michael Cohen.
(Courtesy, American Crafts Council.) (Right)

Unless otherwise noted, all photographs of the author's work by
David Dantzler.
Drawings by Jed Rothwell.

Book design by Mary Frances Gazze

ISBN: 0-385-00120-7
Library of Congress Catalog Card Number 73–92410

To: Betty Rathbun, Enid Norris, Jeremy Norris,
and Vera Westerman for their practical help
and encouragement and
with gratitude to my teachers at Putney Art School,
particularly Tony Benham.

AUTHOR'S NOTE

This book is meant as a starting point. I've tried to avoid being technical and to introduce the reader simply to the pleasures and possibilities of the craft of pottery.

In attempting to describe complicated procedures simply, I may seem to have insulted the reader's intelligence: to say glibly that only intelligent people want to make pots wouldn't be true. I.Q. doesn't come into it at all. We take from pottery what we need and give what we can. The incoherent can express themselves vividly through the medium of clay; the voluble, learn something of silence; and the tense, relax. It's all very therapeutic and fulfilling.

R.Z.

A beautifully shaped earthenware bottle with black matt glaze covered with brown drip decoration by Minoru Nojima. (Courtesy, American Crafts Council.)

CONTENTS

THE JOYS OF POTTERY

"How I would like to pot, but I wouldn't have the talent . . ." Many people have said this to me and I think they meant it. Real talent is rare, but so much can be achieved with perseverance, enjoyment, and hard work that my reason for writing this book is to persuade those who hesitate that they should delay no longer. They should use what opportunities they have for joining that most exciting, satisfying, frustrating—and certainly most addictive—of all crafts—pottery. The slogan "Enrich Your Leisure" is sometimes used to persuade people to join adult education classes. Well, if you do take up pottery, you will have no more leisure, no more boredom. Further, you will have a wonderfully obscure technical language of your own. (I was going to say to bore your acquaintances with, but strangely enough, few people seem bored by the subject.) Perhaps an ideal future lies ahead when the world will be divided not by opposing ideologies, but into those who make pots and those who buy them.

There are not enough handmade pots in the world, so it follows that there aren't enough potters. Although more and more well-designed goods are mass-produced, there is a real hunger for articles with the individuality that machines cannot achieve; articles with the flaws, the deviations from norm that can give life and character to an everyday object. People need pots. You can see that from the way they love to look at them, to handle and to buy. Even work that to the trained eye is clumsy, ill-designed and poorly executed, will, unfortunately, sometimes find a willing buyer. Every year more potters are selling their work, but this does not mean a lowering of standards. Quite the contrary. A well-made pot will stand out on a shelf full of mediocre work; a well-designed piece will soon prove that it is functional as well as beautiful. The loose lid proclaims its intention of falling out when the teapot is tilted; the weak handle suggests it will not support the weight of the full pitcher; a thin rim warns of probable chipping; and who wants a container that is heavy even when empty?

Clay has been taken from the ground and made into pots since the first awakening of civilization. The potter knows

Teapot and goblets by Vally Possony. (Photo by Cynthia Brumback.)

he is part of a continuous process, and although always trying to make something different, he knows that there is nothing new to be made. It has all been done before, many, many times.

There was a recurring myth in early civilizations that man was molded out of clay by God the Creator, who then breathed life into him. Even the description of a pot tallies with that of a human being. A pot has a shoulder, a waist, a neck, a foot, a belly—and the clay mixture from which it is made is called the body.

The growing number of experts with greater technical knowledge, and the increasingly intellectual and sometimes mystical approach of many contemporary potters may obscure a basic fact: To make a pot is a very easy thing to do, it is also relaxing and enjoyable. This is not to belittle work of the highest standard, but to say that the simplicity of the craft should not be lost sight of in the search for excellence.

No book could ever take the place of a teacher. An encouraging "like this . . ." and a demonstration convey so easily what the written word must work hard to do. Ideally the would-be potter should find a class and attend as frequently as possible. But not everyone lives within easy reach of a class and many would-be potters are tied to their homes. To work alone, without companionship and encouragement is not easy, but beginnings are always difficult. A series of limited objectives can take one a surprisingly long way. One of the joys of pottery is that sometimes beginners can and do produce really beautiful work—and remember you need no more than a lump of clay to have the pleasure of making your first pot. I know a young man who, finding himself with a wheel and some clay, but no knowledge of either, worked the whole business out for himself. It took a long time, but he is now well on the way to becoming a professional potter.

Even if you are lucky enough to attend a class, you may not have as much time to spend there as you would like. In a crowded class you might have to wait your turn on the wheel, and wait weeks for pots to be fired. If this frustrates you, ask yourself whether you could not profit more from what you learn at school if you also fixed up a work area at home.

In our overcivilized society, many people feel that man has come too far too fast, losing a lot on the way, and that

Group of ceramic bottles of various shapes, all hand-formed by Claude Conover.

12

14

the individual is swamped. So do not try to cater to the taste of the majority, or copy others. Produce what you really believe in, and what you enjoy making. However, everyone needs to listen carefully to criticism—even if it seldom seems constructive!

Any doubts about your own artistic ability can be quietened by remembering that this is a craft—and a craft can be learned. There are few rules other than those necessitated by the nature of clay. A pot is judged by its appearance and how well it functions, not by how it was made. My advice on how to go about making pots is only meant as a guide to help start you off.

You can start working without a lot of equipment. Even without a kiln to fire your work, you can still enjoy the experience of clay. Don't worry about lack of ideas. The world is full of pots in disguise: water towers, St. Peter's, St. Paul's. Just look around. Once you start thinking about shapes you will see potential pots everywhere. You don't need to live in the country to appreciate the harmony of natural forms—of course, if you do live in a rural area there will be many inspirations for pot shapes and designs in the woods and fields. Ideas will grow from the handling and experience of clay faster than you will have time to deal with them. Look in museums at the work of primitive potters; study contemporary exhibitions and look at and handle any pots you can find. (The reactions of museum attendants when they catch potters handling pots are really deplorable. We should have a special dispensation.)

Technical achievement for its own sake can easily run away with the potter. It is not the smallest, thinnest, largest, fattest, tallest or whatever pots we should aim for, but rather consider the use for which the pot is intended, the proportion and design. Every shape has its size. It is a useful exercise to make the same shape in a wide range of sizes.

Before squeezing the first ball of clay in your hand and starting your first pot, remember that you are handling a substance that has been ground down by time and weather over many centuries from solid rock to the minute particles that unite to form the mass you hold. This should stifle any impatience you may feel that your pot will have to dry slowly, be fired and cool slowly—taking probably about two weeks in the process. It is not such a long time after all. Clay will obey

Hand-formed bowl by Ruth Duckworth. (Photo by Nancy Campbell Harp, Courtesy, American Crafts Council.)

15

A large thrown bowl by Vally Possony. (Photo by Claire Flanders.)
(Right)

Coffee cup and saucer by Harry Horlock Stringer showing sgraffito through slip.

An array of miniature bottles and bowls by the author.
(Photo by David Lomax.)

the pressure of fingers or hand or tool. It can be squashed up and remade; damped down, resquashed, and remade; and even when bone dry it can be reconstituted by soaking in water. And yet you will soon learn that this obedient substance has its own character and will.

Remember, too, that the small particles of clay are also *extremely* difficult to clean up. So don't work, obviously, on an antique inlay table, but rather on an old table or tray and preferably in a shed or over an easily washed floor.

In outline, the process is as follows. Reduced to the simplest terms, a pot is made from clay sufficiently damp to hold its shape without cracking or slumping. When diluted with water to a thick cream, clay is called "slip." When colored, slip is used for decoration—it is also used for making one piece of clay adhere to another. A thinner mixture is called "slurry" and is officially used for lubrication when "throwing"—working on the wheel—but slurry often just happens. Work carelessly with too much water and you will soon find out what I mean.

The pot is allowed to dry slowly until "leather-hard." It will then have lost its "shine," have the appearance of slab chocolate, and be easy to cut and shape. At this stage any handles, lids, spouts and the like should be added. The work is then left to dry out completely, after which it is known as "atmosphere hard." Now it can be fired slowly (never "cooked" or "baked," please) in a kiln (never in an "oven"). Pots or models must be hollow and not too thick at any place, or they will crack or burst in the kiln. Closed-in shapes must always have an air hole or the pressure of heated, expanding air will cause them to shatter. After a temperature of 930° F. (500° C.) is reached, chemical changes will have taken place as a result of the action of heat on clay, resulting in a solid, but porous and still fragile shape. It would need to be fired to a higher temperature to alter the properties it has acquired. Up to the point of firing, the clay could still have been reclaimed by soaking the pot in water. After the first firing, the ware is known as "bisque" or "biscuit."

At this point the "glaze" is added to the surface of the pot, to give it a shiny or matt surface, and the pot refired to a higher temperature to melt the glaze and make the pot stronger. Now the pot is finished—but it could still be refired if necessary.

TOOLS AND MATERIALS

You will have some decisions to make—the problem is one of almost too much choice—as there are so many techniques to try: throwing, modeling, slabbing, working from molds.

There are different *bodies*—mixtures of clay—to work with: rough or smooth, textured or burnished, colored with oxides or used in their natural state—white, buff, yellow, or red. There are choices of *glaze:* matt, shiny, rough, smooth, mottled, crystalline, and endless varieties of color to work for. The beginner is wise to keep things as simple as possible, but the first decision must be whether to make earthenware or stoneware and thus to what temperature you will fire the pots.

Earthenware or Stoneware?

There is no difference in technique between earthenware and stoneware, only in the composition of the body and in the firing temperature. Earthenware is generally potted thinner than stoneware, and is fired to about 2012° F. (1100° C.). Glazes for earthenware are frequently brightly colored and shiny, but many subtle matt glazes can be bought ready-mixed or worked out with a little experimenting. The trend at the moment seems to be away from earthenware and toward stoneware, but this is a great pity. Earthenware is cheaper to produce and more practical for tableware, as it is quieter at meals—knives and forks on the soft glaze don't produce the scratching sound given by the hard surface of stoneware. However, anyone who has made high-fired pots will understand their fascination. There is a feeling of strength in stoneware (I am not referring to weight!) and many people find the subtle colors more satisfying.

One disadvantage of earthenware is that it is slightly porous, and unless a perfect glaze covers the inside of the pot some seepage is likely over a period of time. This won't matter if you are making tableware, but it is obviously impractical to make vases or planters that will leak. The base of pots can be painted with artists' varnish to make them water-proof, but to make non-porous pots you have only to fire to a higher temperature. At 2282° F. (1250° C.) ware is known as stoneware and is non-porous. Of course, it is not quite as simple as this. The kind of clay used is important; some clays will melt at around 2282° F., and if you are mining your own clay, it is well to test a small quantity on a disk of clay you know will stand up to temperature.

Clay can be either "short"; i.e., crumbly and tending to crack when rolled out, or "smooth," when it may be too soft and plastic to work without it collapsing. Too short a clay can be improved by adding a plastic clay such as ball clay or China clay, and too smooth a clay can be roughened or "opened" by the addition of grog (previously fired clay, ground down to small, medium, or coarse particles), sand, or fire clay. Sometimes two clays can be mixed together to give the "feel" you want. It is worth experimenting to find what body suits you.

Potter's merchants specify what temperature the clays they sell will fire to, and thus whether they are suitable for earthenware, stoneware, or porcelain. However, if you buy clay commercially and find it is too colorless, add up to 25 per cent of red clay. Test mixtures before making stoneware pots; the red color of clay is a sign of high iron content, and iron lowers the melting point. To raise the melting point of a body, flint or feldspar can be added. (For detailed information, see Daniel Rhodes' *Clay and Glazes for the Potter* and *Stoneware and Porcelain.*)

An "open" body will be a better medium for modeling, but will dry out more quickly. If you are making ovenware, an open body allows a greater range of expansion and contraction and the pot will better withstand the sudden changes of temperature in the life of a cooking utensil.

To make porcelain, a special body is required, but there are many problems, mainly caused by the high firing temperature of 2372° F. (1300° C.). It is best to gain some experience before tackling high-fired ware.

Low-fired stoneware—2192° F.–2282° F. (1200° C.–1250° C.)—will give soft-colored glazes with a smooth, creamy quality—indeed, firing to this temperature gives many advantages of both earthenware and stoneware, but pots will still be slightly porous. There is certainly less kiln wear and tear, less replacement of elements, and less risk of pots buckling.

Clay can be bought either in powder form or in plastic bags ready-mixed. In practice, it is often too dry or too damp for immediate use, but this can be adjusted. (See page 38.) For the energetic, clay can be dug from the ground, as any gardener complaining of heavy soil will tell you. It is possible to find large deposits to dig, but it is very hard work and rather time consuming. (See page 31.)

Kilns

Once you have clay you can make pots or models, but nothing that will last unless it is fired. Unfired clay is useless for anything but ornament—and very fragile ornaments at that. To fire your work you will need to buy, or build, a kiln. Building a kiln is not a project to undertake lightly, and I would not recommend it to the beginner.*

The first points to consider before buying a kiln are: whether you will be using gas or electricity for power; the size you need; the temperature you require; where you will put it; the access to your source of power, and finally, which way the door opens (a very important point in a small space). Many kilns are top loading. These kilns are cheaper to buy and save space, but are more tricky to load. (See page 129.) The advantages of a gas-fired kiln are many—no elements to burn through, and the joys of reduction firing. (See page 139.) However, the initial cost is considerably higher. You may have a problem fixing a flue and possible complaints from the neighbors about the smoke when you indulge in reduction firing. Kilns are also run on bottled gas, and diesel oil is a cheap form of fuel, but again the initial cost is high.

Of course, the fuel used by the old potters was wood, but that is hardly a practicable suggestion today, even if you do live on the edge of a forest, as it involves two to three days and nights spent stoking. In Africa, even today, pots are fired to a low temperature in a pit in the ground, using bushes and leaves as fuel; but if you wish to indulge in an open-air firing, try a raku kiln. (See page 147.)

For the beginner who is not yet sure what he or she will make, or even how much time there will be to work, an

* Information given in *A Potter's Book* by Bernard Leach and in H. Fraser and L. Ceram's *Kilns and Kiln Firing*.

electric kiln is really the answer. There are many different designs and sizes on the market. As with most consumer goods, you will get what you pay for, and it is foolish to try to economize with the most important item of your equipment. If you want to buy a second-hand kiln, remember that removal is expensive and difficult, and the brickwork may be damaged if it is not very carefully handled. Also find out how many firings it has had and to what temperature it has been fired—consistent high firings will result in the elements (the wire coils through which the electricity runs) being weakened. (This can easily be seen if the coils are unevenly spaced or bunched up.) Also, severe cracks in the brickwork would have to be filled in or heat loss might eventually damage the kiln insulation and would add considerably to the initial cost.

It is hard to advise what size kiln is best to buy. Small kilns are initially cheaper, but more expensive to run. Not only do they use comparatively more electricity, but the smaller space is more wasteful to pack. If you produce a lot of work or want to make large pieces, it can be very frustrating to be restricted by kiln space. On the other hand, an empty waiting kiln may well tempt you to keep everything you make just to fill it up and have a firing. This situation tends to discourage self-criticism and may lead to a lot of unwanted pots. It is, however, always better to fire fairly frequently as you will learn more quickly from mistakes and get much needed experience with glaze testing. Sharing a kiln with friends can be a solution.

There are very small kilns on the market for testing glazes, but as they fire very rapidly and the behavior of glazes is largely dependent on the length of firing time, results in these little kilns are not always true.

Make sure that the kiln you choose will fire to the temperature you require. Some kiln makers advertise their kilns as firing to a stated *cone* number, which can be confusing as there are different cones on the market. (See page 128.) It is the actual temperature to which the kiln will fire that you need to know. Again, low-temperature kilns are considerably cheaper to buy than high-temperature kilns.

Where to place the kiln must be carefully considered: If you have no proper workroom, perhaps you have a spare room or dry outside shed. However, check that the electric supply is adequate and properly wired. Our first kiln spent a year on the top landing and was most useful for airing the washing and generally warming the house. However, the next kiln had a noisy thermostat, and the switch clicking on and off all night would have kept the whole family awake. It is obviously unwise to keep inflammable material on top of kilns, but they are well-insulated and quite safe, provided reasonable precautions are taken and the wiring is in good order.

Once you have a kiln, the possibility of selling your work becomes real, and it is easy to argue that one is not just spending money, but actually saving it. To those who wish to sell, either from financial need or as a justification of their work, remember that there are grave disadvantages in selling before you are really ready—you may promise to produce something slightly beyond your ability, with the resultant nerve strain, or you may find yourself making endless coffee sets when you really yearn to make fountains. There is a great demand for good tableware, and fortunate is the potter who enjoys making it.

Wheels

To make thrown pots you will need a wheel. Many potters are happy coiling, slabbing or working with molds, but if you can get a wheel, please do—throwing is not easy to learn, but it is the most satisfying and enjoyable technique. But don't get the idea that thrown pots are the highest form of pottery—the aristocrats of clay. Anyone with this idea should go and look at the work of those early potters who never knew the wheel: The Aztecs, Mexicans, Peruvians, who produced splendid pots using coiling and pinching techniques.

An electric wheel saves energy and will enable you to throw bigger pots more quickly, but it is of course much more expensive to buy. The peace of working on a silent kick wheel where you provide the "power," should not be ignored—sometimes haste and efficiency are worth sacrificing. This simple piece of machinery can be made by a good handyman.* With a kick wheel you quickly learn to regulate the speed of kicking to the immediate needs of pot and

* See Murray Fieldhouse's *Pottery*.

The potter working with an electric wheel.

hands. For any form of decoration or coloring that runs round a pot, a kick wheel will give better results than a hand banding wheel, and it is also much easier for turning pots.

Tools

The human being is already equipped with the best tools in the world, they don't fall on the floor or get lost in the slurry: hands and fingers. Unfortunately, the more you pot the shorter your nails will become, and you will lose their valuable cutting and scraping edges. A few suggested additions:

GENERAL WORK

A really sharp, thin-bladed knife.

Large plastic sponges for cleaning up, one for glaze and one for clay.

Sieves: 60-mesh for clay; 60–120-mesh for glaze.

A metal "kidney": A flexible kidney-shaped piece of flat metal, invaluable for scraping off guilty unevenness, smoothing away unwanted throwing rings, tidying the base of a pot, etc.

Wire for wedging, etc.: Nylon wire is long lasting and good for cutting clay for wedging, but wire for slabbing, trimming clay in molds and cutting pots off the wheelhead needs to be finer and less bouncy. Twisted wire can be bought on a reel, and lengths are cut with a wire cutter. Toggles or large buttons can be tied on each end for handles.

Lidded plastic bins or buckets to store clay and glazes. Clay improves with keeping and is cheaper to buy in large batches. You will also need a separate bin for slurry; the clay particles sink to the bottom and can be reclaimed and dried out on plaster or biscuit slabs.

Scales: An old pair of kitchen scales will serve well for weighing clay, but a special gram scale for glazes can be bought from pottery suppliers.

Bats: Pieces of square or round hard board or asbestos on which to dry pots. Asbestos is more absorbent and gives quicker drying. It is useful to learn to throw on bats. (See page 68.)

Special tools needed for potting:
A) Cutting wire
B) Calipers
C) Metal kidney
D) Banding wheel or whirler
E) Turning and modeling tools
F) Throwing bat

Plastic ruler and protractor: Very useful for measuring if you have difficulty getting handles and spouts in line.

Calipers for measuring: If you make tableware, you will need several calipers permanently set for lids, saucers, etc. Produce

work of the same size and you will always be able to replace a broken lid. If you don't want a lot of equipment around, use only one pair of calipers and constantly reset them to the measurement required, keeping a record of the various sizes.

A paint scraper: For cleaning wedging table and wheelhead.

A banding wheel or whirler: A small wheel turned by hand, invaluable for modeling, coiling, glaze decoration, or just simply as a means of rotating your work to observe it from all angles.

Oil: Don't forget the oilcan. Any mechanical moving part must be oiled regularly, or it will cease to move.

MODELING, SLABBING, COILING

Wooden modeling tools—metal ones will rust unless you cherish them; stainless steel tools are expensive.

Two (or more) wooden sticks ⅜″ thick, about 2″ wide and up to 12″ long.

A rolling pin: For slabbing and beating.

A hollow tool for cutting small holes. An umbrella rib or quill will serve, or a special tool can be bought. Plastic drinking straws can also be used.

THROWING

A soft, natural sponge, small enough to hold comfortably in the hand: Used on the wheel to mop up surplus slip and to trim the rim of the pot. A piece of chamois leather gives a smooth rim, but is very apt to disappear into the slurry, unless tied to the wheel with string.

A small piece of sponge fastened onto a short stick with wire or string: To get the slurry out of tall thin pots.

A cutting needle with a handle, or a darning needle stuck in a cork.

Turning tools: Best bought with a good-sized, rounded handle, to give a good grip. Tools can be cut from bamboo cane with a sharp knife and shaped to your requirements.

A rubber "kidney": For throwing smooth pots, inside or out. Casseroles in particular are easier to wash when made without throwing ridges inside. Also very useful for scraping the last drops of glaze from containers.

FOR RAKU FIRING

Long-handled tongs and asbestos gloves.

Before you start to work, a few basic rules: Think hard what you are going to do and how you are to do it; work carefully and as cleanly as possible; never hurry or try to speed up any stage in the chain of processes; avoid sharp edges on your pots—they will chip; check all stages of work and dry everything slowly; never despair—a degree of despair can add drama to an exasperating day, but should not be indulged in to excess as it is, obviously, non-productive.

It will save trouble and needless repetition if careful records are kept of what you do and how you do it. A large notebook with numbered pages and an index to those pages makes this easier. Keeping clay and glaze out of this book is harder than keeping a cook book clean—I've no suggestions other than making rough notes and transcribing them later away from the work surface.

And a word about tidiness and cleanliness in work. (I hear the raucous laughs of my old workshop companions, but I did learn the hard way—indeed the peculiar qualification I have for writing this book is that I have probably made every mistake possible through carelessness, haste, and excess of zeal.)

Workbenches should always be kept clean, tools carefully wiped after use. Little bits of hard clay can cause serious trouble if allowed to get into throwing clay—a dirty tool is a very inefficient one. Lumps of clay, flint, dirt, or whatever, however small, in the glaze bucket will settle on glazed pots, and give you the terrible decision of whether to wash off all the glaze, sieve the whole batch and start again (a time-consuming process) or try to patch up the mess (generally a mistake). Always keep glaze ingredients clean, dry, and clearly labeled. Feldspar instead of flint painted on kiln shelves will ensure your pots adhering to the shelves when fired to stoneware temperature. (The melting point of feldspar is considerably lower than that of flint.) A wrong ingredient in the glaze could cause all the glaze to run off the pots with the same result. If any glaze ingredient is wet, this will affect its weight, and you will not get the planned result.

Try to train yourself to put the same tool in the same place when working and you will save hours vaguely looking for things—clay will camouflage any tool very efficiently.

Be brave handling raw pots; the nervous shake can cause as much trouble for the beginner as a careless or hurried movement. You will quickly learn the necessary combination of strength and sensitivity of touch. It is better to grasp pots firmly with one or both hands than to try to pick them up with finger and thumb.

Practice drawing what you want to make, and what other people have made. It is helpful to get a planned shape down on paper and consider the proportions and how any proposed decoration will affect the whole. It is especially valuable when making pots composed of several different parts to make a plan showing where sections will be joined, where extra strength will be needed, etc. However, if the beautiful pots you dream of depress you on paper, you may just be very bad at drawing—then you must "draw in clay." But don't give up pencil and paper altogether, try graph paper, using the lines to help you draw the right shape. And keep trying.

Remember that any slight flaw in a new pot will be intensified at every stage. A tiny crack will open as the pot dries and is fired, and any unevenness will become more and more obvious. Once a pot is fired, no mistake or carelessness can be rectified, and although the work may be praised, you will know better. It is easy, though, to fail to see the quality of something you have made because it does not come out of the kiln exactly as planned. Indeed, it is a good idea to put away a disappointing pot, then take it out again and look at it when your original gloom is forgotten. You may be surprised. Or give it to an unsuspecting friend you don't often see, and you may find yourself long afterward wondering who made such an interesting piece. This practice, of course, works both ways—you may be horrified at what you once made. But I should like to stress that desire for success is not the best reason for starting to pot—much more important is the sheer pleasure of burying your arms in the slurry. If this makes you shudder, then put the book down, quick. If, on the other hand, you are one of those who enjoys mud between the toes, your first necessity is to buy a bag of clay.

MAKING A START

There is plenty of clay lying around in the ground, especially by river banks and on the sites of old rivers, but unless you have lots of time and energy don't rely on natural sources for your main supply. However, it is very rewarding to fire clay you have found yourself and compare the behavior of different natural clays and their effect on glazes—I should say *under* glazes. Small amounts can be worked in the fingers and either made into pinch pots (page 40) or thrown on the wheel—it will be easy to remove any stones or impurities by hand. In the glaze firing, put these little pots inside another pot, or on an old piece of kiln shelf, as they may melt at your usual firing temperature. You can then consider whether you want to use the clay for a slip glaze or as a glaze ingredient instead of using it as a body.

When preparing clay for use, dig it as free from earth, roots, and stones as possible and spread it out to dry in the open. When it crumbles easily, crush it to powder, using a pestle and mortar. If you are processing large amounts this could be a slow job, so use a mallet or other crushing tool. Then stir in water to make a thin slurry and strain the mixture through a coarse sieve (60-mesh). Allow the clay to settle for several hours before draining off as much water as possible. Coarse sacking tied over a bucket will make a rough-and-ready sieve. Scrape the clay onto the sacking and leave it to drip. When it is a solid mass it can be put on a plaster or biscuit bat until dry enough to use. You see the advisability of testing a sample to make sure the clay is suitable for use before embarking on such a project. Incidentally, all clay is best stored out of doors where the weather will mature it. In ancient China, potters would lay down a field of clay for their heirs to use, but this is hardly a practical suggestion in our urban society.

Clay is prepared for work by kneading and wedging.

Kneading

Start with a small amount of clay until you have mastered the basic movements of kneading. The clay is held in

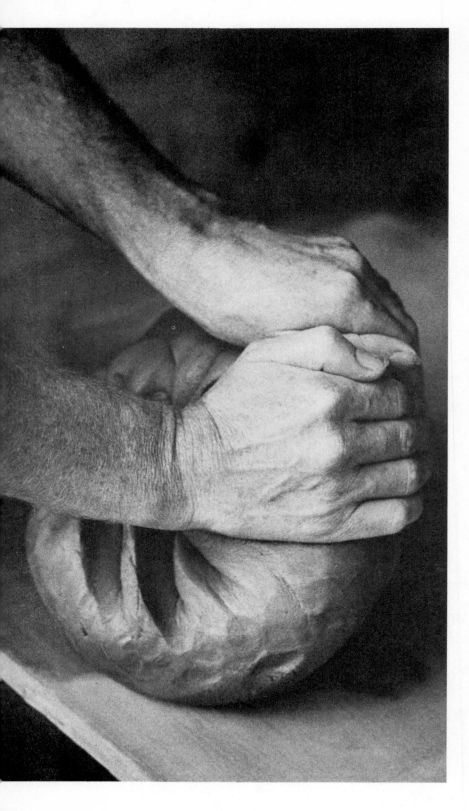

Kneading. The clay is held in both hands, one supporting the main weight while the other stretches and folds the clay until it is thoroughly mixed.

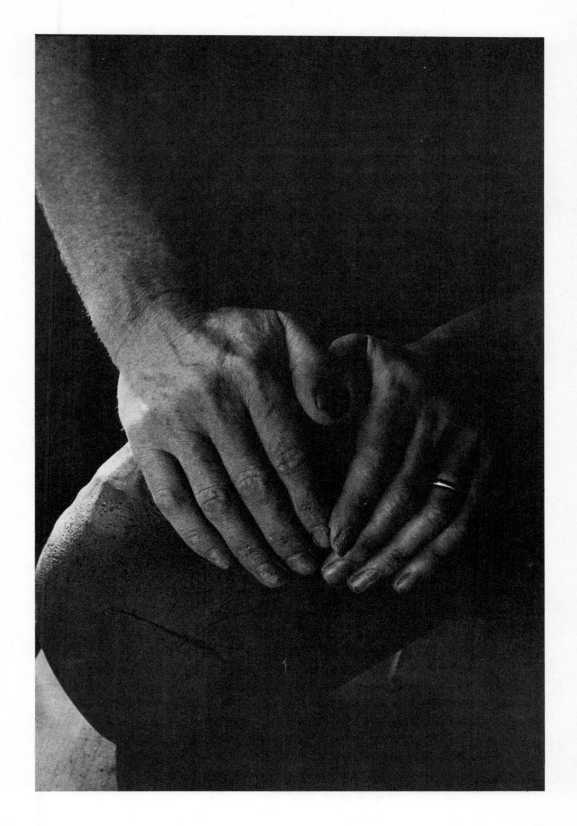

The spiral pattern formed in the clay by the action of kneading.

34

both hands and rotated with a circular movement, one hand supporting the main weight while the other stretches and folds the clay over on itself. A spiral pattern is formed in the mass while the kneading proceeds and the clay becomes thoroughly mixed. Ideally the clay should be kept in a round shape, but it may tend to lengthen out into a roll. Then you can pick it up, and bang it down lengthwise to get it back into shape. Not only does kneading mix the clay thoroughly, done properly it also forces out all the air. However, the advantage of wedging is that you can see what progress the clay is making and do not have to rely on "feel."

Wedging

Careful wedging (or thorough kneading) is of utmost importance for throwing, but it is also important for slabbing —(making pots from rolled out slabs of clay) especially if slabs are cut in bulk. (See page 45.) The object is to mix the clay thoroughly and to get rid of all pockets of air, foreign bodies, small stones, etc. No beginner should attempt to throw unless the clay is just right for them—some prefer it stiffish, especially for larger pieces; others like it to be considerably softer. It is up to you to experiment and find what you work with best. Soft clay is much easier to center and work on the wheel, but will collapse, or become "tired" more quickly.

When wedging you will need a strong wire or nylon cord with a handle on each end large enough to give a good grip. It is very important to have a firm, strong table with a good surface that will not flake off into the clay, and at a comfortable height at which to work. A slab of marble is good for wedging on, some people like a thick slab of plaster of paris (but this will tend to dry out the clay), or a piece of hard board is good, or even a strong piece of sacking nailed over a wooden surface.

Start with the largest amount of clay you can comfortably handle, since the greater the weight you bang down, the faster the air will be forced out. Beat the lump of clay into a rough wedge shape, then, with the high end of the edge toward you on the edge of the table, draw the wire across, cutting the clay in half. Lift the top half and inspect

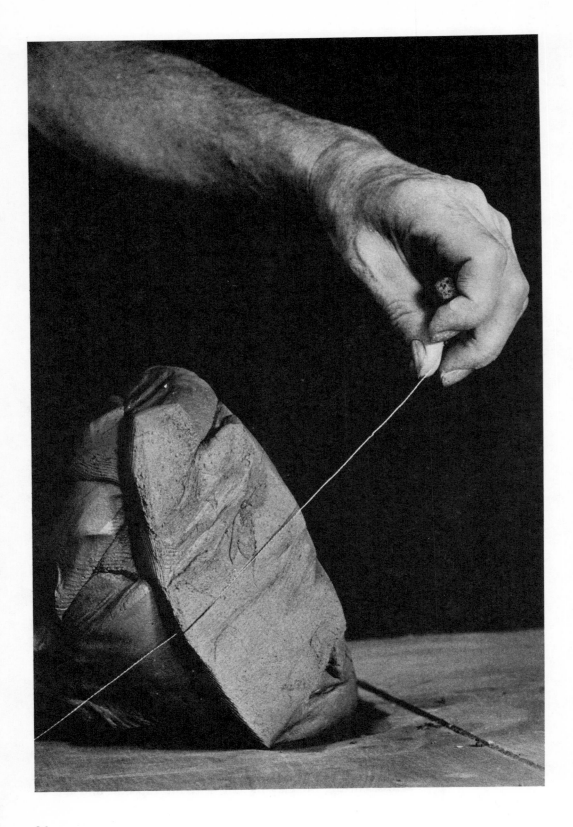

Cutting the clay in
half for wedging. (Left)

Banging the top half
of the clay wedge down
on the sharp edge of
the other half.

37

the cut sections. Note the appearance of the clay at this stage, remove any pieces of stone or foreign matter, and smooth out any air pockets. Then lift the top half with *flat* hands (don't dig your fingers in), turn it over, lift it right above your head and bang it down with conviction on the sharp edge of the piece left on the table. Keep both hands on the clay until you have brought it right down; *don't* drop it. You might miss. Then pick up the entire mass, and turn it so that the section which was underneath is now on top, and so that the next cut will run at right angles to the first. Smooth any rough edges; it is possible to catch more air when wedging than you force out. Now repeat the process until the cut surface feels smooth and regular when you run your finger over it, and no irregular lines or bumps appear when you compress the mass with both hands. It may take some time, but the process can be very enjoyable once you get into the rhythm. However, particles of clay can spatter a surprising distance and catch the unwary worker a stinging blow. Each time you pick up the wire, run finger and thumb along it to remove any bits it may have caught on its passage through the clay. (Interval for horror stories from people who didn't notice their wire was frayed).

If the clay is stiff it will be very difficult to work. Before wedging, slice it up with the wire and dampen the slices with a sponge, or dip them in water. A few hours soaking may be necessary if the clay is really stiff. If the clay is too wet, knead it on a porous surface; i.e., a plaster-of-paris slab or an old kiln shelf, (or a new one, if you are prepared to wash it down and dry it again before the firing). Clay should be soft enough for the two halves to integrate when banged together. Never bang clay hard with your hands; vigorous slapping can affect their sensitivity and doesn't help the clay particularly.

When you are satisfied with the state of the clay, form it into a neat, oblong shape by banging it onto the table, first one side then the other—again being careful not to catch air in any folds or to bang it down so hard that it sticks to the table.

Always cover clay when not actually wedging, throwing, or kneading. It is surprising how quickly the outer surface will dry, thus wasting all your hard work. Use a sheet of plastic or a damp cloth, as dry cloth will absorb moisture from the clay.

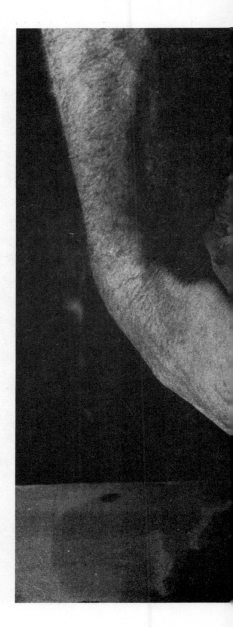

Turning the clay before cutting it again.

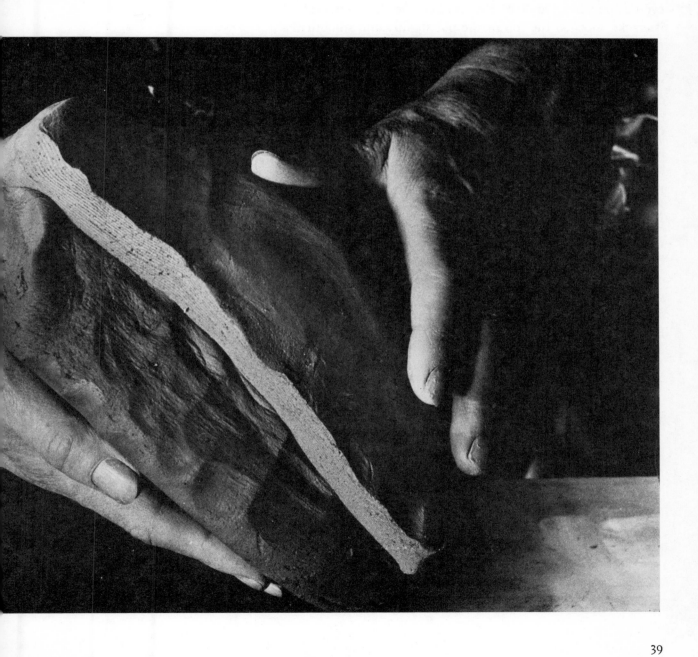

Pinch Pots

The simplest pot in the world to make is a pinch pot. Roll some clay in your palms into a ball. Then, holding it in the left hand, press your thumb into the clay while turning the ball, forming a depression. Deepen this depression while simultaneously pinching the side to thin the walls. Make the sides and top of the pot as level as possible and the walls as even as possible. Don't let the rim become thin and weak; if it cracks, moisten the top of the pot slightly and smooth the rim well over.

With practice, larger pinch pots can be made on a banding wheel and both hands used to thin the walls. These pots can be made several inches high. Two or more pinch pots can be joined together when leather-hard. Score the edges to be joined with a knife and moisten them with slurry. Then press the parts together, blending the joined sections with fingers or tool. Remember you must always have an air hole so the pot will not crack when drying, or explode when firing. (Air expands when heated, which is one reason for that careful wedging.) However, it is not necessary to wedge before making a pinch pot, as the clay is well enough worked with the hands. Many shapes can be made by this method. Holes can be cut to give interest, textures can be imprinted on the surface. You may even get hung up on pinch pots and want to spend your time exploiting their possibilities. For bigger pots, the coiling method is just as enjoyable, but you begin to need some equipment.

Making a pinch pot.

A pinch pot of stoneware by Ed Oshier. (Photo by Milmoe, courtesy, American Crafts Council.)

Coiling

For coiling you will need two sticks, a cloth, and a rolling pin to roll out the base. But first decide what size and shape you want to make and the size of the base required. Take a bat, lay your cloth on this, then your piece of clay on the cloth, with the sticks on either side. Beat the clay roughly flat with your hands and finally, using the rolling pin, roll it out, using the sticks to ensure that you roll an even slab. Any round object of the required size will do to cut around to give you a base. Roll sausages of clay between your hands, or between flat of hand and table, as evenly as possible and at least ½" thick. Coil the sausages one after another along the edge of the base and up on top of each other, working round and round. Several coils can be worked together at once to form a continuous wall, or each coil smoothed into place separately. Between the base of the pot and the first coil, work in a very narrow sausage of clay to strengthen this point. The outside surface can be left as it stands, smoothed over, or marked with a different texture. The inside must be carefully smoothed over to ensure that the finished pot will not leak. It is easier to start with a cylindrical shape while you are learning how the clay behaves. Very large pots can be coiled, but you will need to support the structure with a bandage or cloth when it shows the slightest sign of sagging, then leave the pot to harden before continuing. If the pot has widened too much toward the top, cut a V-shaped section out and work the cut pieces together again.

A thickly coiled pot can be beaten out into a fatter, rounder shape by using a stone or a rounded piece of wood in one hand inside the pot, a flat piece of wood in the other hand outside the pot, and beating the wall thinner.

Flat strips of clay, instead of sausages, can be used for coiling. This is quicker but initially more difficult to master. It is also easier if making a bigger pot to use a biscuited pot or even tight rolls of newspaper as a support. Newspaper will burn away, but you must check, if using any other support, that you will be able to extract it without damaging the new pot—remember that clay shrinks as it dries. It's a good idea to wrap newspaper or a cloth round the mold to prevent the new pot sticking to it.

Coiling is also a good method for making models if the

shape is pretty simple. Another method is to make the model from a solid lump of clay. When it is leather-hard, cut it carefully in half and scoop out the interior, leaving the wall of the model not more than ½″ thick. Then join the two pieces together again with slip. Don't forget an air hole.

The beginning of a coiled pot. (Photo by Cynthia Brumback.)

A finished coiled stoneware pot by Ruth Duckworth. (Photo by Aidron Duckworth, courtesy, American Crafts Council.)

Slabbing

It is now a short step to slabbing—an excellent method for making square or oblong pots—just a larger amount of clay to roll out. You must watch for the exact state of dryness when pieces can be handled without distortion but are not yet dry enough to crack. With slab pots you cannot work freehand as with coiling—you must work out exact measurements and cut out a template (pattern) from stiff paper or cardboard (worth labeling and saving for future use). Round, square, and oblong pots can be slabbed, even pots with lids can be made with this method. Very slow drying is advised for slabbed pots of any size; the risk of warping is much higher than with thrown work. Allow the rolled-out clay to dry slightly before putting the template on and cutting round it—a very sharp, thin knife is best for this. Use a ruler on top of the template to hold it in place if it tends to slip as you cut, and cut straight; if the knife is held at an angle your piece won't fit. Joins are made in the usual way—the edges scored, coated thinly with slip, and pressed evenly to ensure adhesion. Strengthen all joins with a thin roll of clay pressed well into the inner angle and smoothed over. If the shape of the pot becomes distorted when assembling the parts, don't worry. The pot can be beaten straight with a stick when the joins have hardened and the whole structure is firmer.

For large slabbed pots, there is a simple method of cutting several slabs at once. You will need several sticks of equal thickness and length and a much larger amount of well-wedged clay. Use exactly the same method for rolling out as above, except that you will use several sticks (obviously, an equal number) piled up each side of the lump of clay. When the clay is rolled out and quite smooth on top, remove the top stick from each side and run the wire carefully along what will now be the top sticks. This will cut an even slab of clay. Repeat the process, laying out the slabs to harden. To move the slabs, hook one end over the rolling pin and lift. You may need a helper to support the sticks as you cut, but this method saves a lot of time and trouble and is well worth persevering with.

*Rolling out the clay in preparation for making slabbed pots. (Above)
Cutting several slabs at once. (Below)*

A more unusual slabbed vase with foot by Theodore Randall. (Courtesy, American Crafts Council.) (Right)

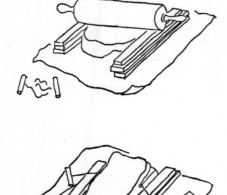

Slabbed Pots from Molds

The purpose of a mold is to support clay in a particular form until it has dried enough to hold the shape. Molds also let one repeat the same piece as many times as desired.

Plaster of paris is porous, and pots made in these molds will dry rapidly. It is easy to make your own plaster of paris shapes,* but plaster is tricky and must be used with great care by potters. Even a small piece of plaster in the clay will draw moisture from the atmosphere and swell. This will cause the pot to crack or break even after stoneware firing. Many potters' merchants sell plaster of paris molds in a variety of shapes and sizes, and the time and worry saved in buying these may be worth the expense.

When using a mold, check that the inner surface is free from small particles of clay. Pick up the slab of clay with the rolling pin as described above and lay it gently in the mold, using the sponge to press it in place. Surplus clay should be cut off with a wire. Hold the wire straight and run it along the top of the mold to cut a straight rim. If the mold is completely dry, the pot will be leather-hard within a few hours. Tip it carefully out of the mold. The edges will be rough, trim them with a sharp knife or hacksaw blade and smooth the rim with a damp sponge. Large dishes should be dried slowly, or they will warp.

A biscuited pot will serve as an efficient mold, the surface being sufficiently porous to dry the clay without their sticking together. But remember that if clay is drying *round* any mold, the clay will shrink and the mold will not. Unless the shape of the mold is such that the clay merely shrinks *away* from it, sooner or later the clay must crack. Be sure to remove the mold before this happens.

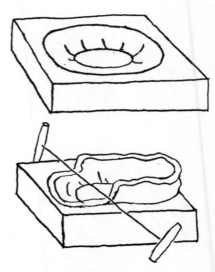

Slabbing in a mold.

Large stones can be used, but there will be difficulty with the clay sticking to them unless they are used when fairly dry or material or paper is laid between stone and clay. Here you will be making the actual pot upside down, so remember to flatten the bottom or add small pads of clay for feet so that it will stand properly.

The simplest of all molds is a cardboard box, or a tray of expanded polystyrene, into which clay can be pressed or,

* Detailed information in Dora Billington's, *The Technique of Pottery.*

46

if the box is large enough, slabs of clay fitted. When the pot is leather-hard, simply tip it out of the box and tidy the back of the pot with a knife and sponge the edges. Alternatively, the box can be inverted and the clay applied over it. Mailing tubes have great possibilities for making long, thin pots on.

Slabbed Pots on Balloons

Children's balloons make excellent forms on which to base a slabbed pot. Blow the balloon reasonably firm, but not as hard as it will go, or it may pop when pressure is applied. Place the balloon in the mouth of a jam jar, or other container while rolling out enough clay to cover it. Use a tape measure to measure the size. Cut the clay out in a clover shape if the balloon is round. Now fit the clay over the balloon, join the edges carefully and stand it back in its holder. If making an open shape, the inside can be smoothed over when the balloon is removed. The critical decision is when to prick the balloon—too soon and the pot will sink with an exhausted sigh; too late, and the pot will have cracked. When you have successfully completed this operation remember to flatten the base. Now is the time to coil neck, lip, or lid, or to texture the pot.

Beating

A method of shaping coiled, thrown, or balloon pots is "beating." When the pot is leather-hard, but not so dry that the rim will crack, it can be beaten into shape either with a stick or with a flat tool that will also give a texture to the surface. These tools can be made from wooden spoons or flat pieces of wood bound with rope or string, or carved with designs.

Slabbing is an excellent technique for making boxes, or small quantities of tiles. However, if you want to decorate tiles in a big way, it's better to buy ready-made plain ones in bulk, then glaze and refire them. The process of making a large batch of tiles is tedious. Thin tiles tend to buckle and their shape makes even drying difficult—the edges dry first and curl up. Scoring the reverse side will help prevent this.

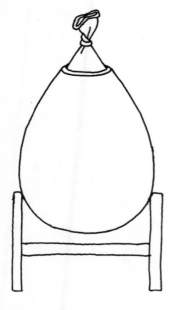

Balloon pot supported in a container for the clay to dry.

LEARNING TO THROW

Anyone with any experience of potting agrees that it is not easy to learn to throw, but those who can throw agree that it is the most enjoyable and satisfying activity. Generally speaking, the young, strong, and confident have a better chance of mastering a difficult art quickly, but when the rewards are so great it is well worth putting a great deal of effort into learning—unless actually crippled with rheumatism. The art of throwing lies in balance and control, not brute strength; many physically small potters throw very big pots. Throwing is also the quickest way to make pots. A good potter can throw sixty an hour, and that is not the record.

If you want to learn to throw well, concentrate on your goal. Don't waste time firing second-rate pots, cut them in half to see what progress you are making. Work systematically with the same weight of clay making the same shape, mastering the cylinder before progressing to the bowl, and do not be side-tracked.

But if you want to enjoy yourself on the long road, you can have a lot of fun with thrown work. A collapsed pot may suggest an animal shape; the uneven ridges of an intact pot can be textured off, or the pot can be beaten into a strong, interesting form. When beating a round pot into a square or oval shape make sure the base is not distorted or it will have to be cut out and replaced with one with right shape, using the slabbing method.

Before rejecting a pot look for any virtues it may have. Are you avoiding the struggle of cutting a footring on an off-center bowl, when you feel that if you persevered it could be a successful pot? Technical perfection is not the only criterion: Try to see each piece for what it is, not what it failed to be. The virtues of vitality and spontaneity can be lost in the struggle for perfection.

Once the initial difficulties of throwing have been mastered, always plan and draw pots before starting on the wheel. Be quite sure of what you want to make, and don't dither —indecision is quickly communicated to the hands. Most enjoyable and relaxing is to throw with a completely open mind and let the wheel form the shape, but this, of course, needs a certain degree of proficiency. First you must learn to throw.

If your wheel has no seat attached, take trouble to find a stool or box the right height for you to sit comfortably and avoid undue fatigue.

You will need a bowl of slurry, a turning tool or piece of wood for trimming the base of the pot, a soft sponge (a natural one is more sensitive), a needle for cutting off any uneven rims and a wire for cutting pots off the wheelhead. And, of course, a wheel.

Always work with well-wedged clay, and always weigh the clay before throwing. This "well-wedged" cannot be emphasized too strongly. It is essential for a good pot, and for a beginner it is essential for a pot at all. Cut the block of well-wedged clay into squares of a pound weight (a good size to start with, unless you have very large, strong hands, when you will do better with a larger ball). Pat these squares into neat balls with rounded hands.

Make sure everything is within reach before starting work. (It is irritating to have to wipe the slurry off your hands and go in search of the bats I forgot to mention in the previous paragraph.) Also, is there plenty of space within easy reach to put your pots on? Have a cloth handy to wipe your hands.

Now moisten the wheelhead slightly to ensure adhesion, then "throw" (i.e., drop with force) the ball of clay as near to the center as possible; on some wheelheads you'll have a series of concentric rings to help you.* This takes a bit of practice, but if you miss the center badly ease the clay over, being careful not to catch air between clay and wheelhead in the process. Air is the potter's main enemy on the wheel; try to avoid trapping it. Start the wheel at top speed if using an electric model. If using a kick wheel, then kick as fast as you can. The potter's wheel goes round counter-clockwise in the West; in Japan it runs clockwise. Dampen your hands with slurry or water and tackle the hardest part of the whole business: centering. This means getting the clay running exactly true in the center of the wheelhead, and is achieved by wrapping both hands right around and over the ball of clay and pressing down and in until you feel the clay running evenly and your hands cease to jump.

If the wheel has a raised rim, use this as an arm support;

* If your wheelhead has no rings, use a sharp metal tool, over the wheel and bring the tool into contact with the wheelhead to score your own rings—they help a lot.

if it doesn't, then hold your arms firmly to your body at the elbows or thighs. Use both hands as much as possible as one tool—hold them together and you will have more control. Sometimes greater control can be obtained by wrapping the left hand round the clay and using the right hand to strengthen the left wrist. If, however, you find the clay jumps more and more, then you are pushing it off center with too much force. Use a more even pressure. Stop the wheel and push it back to the center. (Watch for air again.) If you get really desperate in your efforts to get the clay on center (and it is useless to proceed unless you do so) then you must cheat and use a turning tool to cut the base true. But first ask yourself if you are throwing with clay too stiff or improperly wedged; or are you too tired or tense to work properly? Would you be happier with a slower wheel? Try it. It is easy to "get in a state" when learning to center, but don't feel you have failed if you have to resort to the turning tool; once you have gained control of the clay you will soon master this first and most difficult phase.

Several ways of holding your hands to center the clay in the middle of the wheelhead. For greatest control, use both hands as one tool.

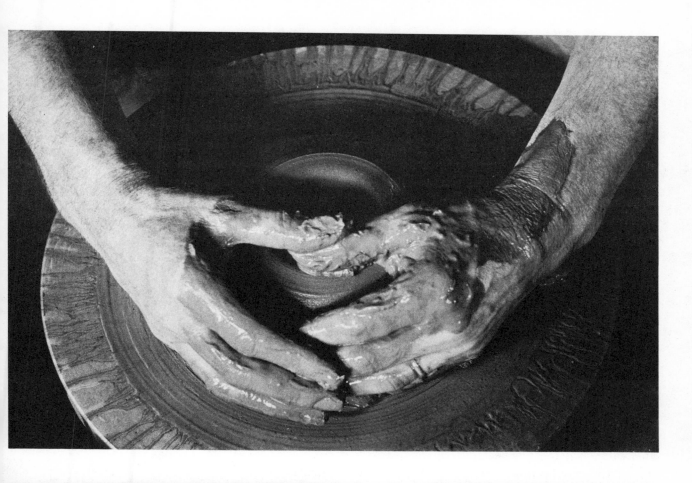

When throwing, always keep a thin film of moisture over hands and clay, but avoid puddles. These puddles will quickly become absorbed and form pockets of much wetter, unmanageable clay. Also, keep the wheelhead clean: A bump of clay will cause your hands to jump. It is well to avoid getting in a mess by not letting the slurry build up in the well of the wheel. Wipe the rim clean frequently and wipe your hands if you get too messy. Always move your hands carefully, don't jerk away from the clay, or it will be knocked off center.

Assuming that the piece is centered, the next step is to "cone" the clay. This, as the name implies, means squeezing it up into a cone shape with both hands, using a firm inward and upward pressure. The object is to mix the clay thoroughly and make it more plastic. Successful coning has rather the action of a volcano—the clay is forced up from the center of the mass, then pushed down the outside as the cone is pressed down to a ball shape. This process should force air out of the clay, but done too vigorously, with too much "overhang" over the side of the cone, it will catch air instead. Avoid this by using the greater strength of your thumb bases to press the cone down and your fingers to control the descending clay in a smooth line. Press the clay down to a door knob shape, which will give you more control of the vital area where clay meets wheel.

If the clay becomes hot (don't laugh, you can generate a lot of heat through friction) or remains obstinately the same shape, you are probably pressing too hard, have the clay too stiff, or are not using enough lubrication.

Now to start producing a pot. Wrap both hands round the ball of clay, thumbs over the center, steadying the right thumb with the left thumb, and press it gently down into the center of the ball. This pressure will combine with the movement of the wheel to form a hole down the center of the pot. Continue pressing until you judge your thumb is about ½" from the wheelhead, then stop the wheel and use the needle to check the depth.

Assuming the base is the right thickness—and if it is much too thick then you can press further and make the hole deeper—with your hands in the same position as for making the hole, "open up" the pot. The right thumb should be pushed down inside and your hands wrapped round the pot, with left thumb still steadying the right. Push gently

Coning. Push the clay up into a cone shape with both hands using a firm inward and upward pressure.

Coning down. To force air out of the clay, clay is pushed down the outside as the cone is pressed down to a ball shape. (Left)

Opening up the pot. (Right)

54

away from the center with the right thumb, steadying the wall of the pot as you do so. This forms the base of the pot, so get the width right. The wheel should still be running fast, but this is something to experiment with—not everyone finds a fast wheel easy to work on.

Once you have opened out the pot, slow the wheel to half speed and start to thin the walls. You must still use both hands together and keep a thin film of lubrication over hands and clay. Never allow your fingers to slide aimlessly over the pot; this will only weaken and distort the walls. Holding your

Knuckling. With left hand inside and right hand outside, thin the walls and begin to shape the pot.

Steady the rim of the pot, after you have reached the top of the wall.

left hand inside the pot and your right hand outside, link your hands by steadying the left thumb with your right knuckle. In fact, this stage of throwing is sometimes called "knuckling." Starting right at the base of the pot, with your fingers exactly opposite each other on either side of the wall, grasp the clay with a firm, even pressure and gently pull it up. It is essential to maintain an even pressure and to pull up at a steady rate. You should feel the clay moving in your hands, and remain in complete control of the movement. When you reach the top of the wall of the pot, always steady the rim, us-

ing left thumb and forefinger each side of the rim, and the right forefinger on top. An uneven rim will soon, by its motion, send the whole pot off-center.

A strong, firm rim on a pot is much less likely to chip and warp than a thin, weak one. It also gives a stronger appearance to the pot. Work on the rim before you have finished pulling up the wall of the pot. Compress the clay with your finger tips. If, however, you find you have pulled the rim up too thin and weak to do this, keep the wheel running and fold the top half inch of the clay outward, over and down, squeezing the air out as you do so. Any projecting edge of clay left by this folding action can be gently worked down

Strengthening the rim of the pot.

into the wall of the pot, or cut away with a tool. You should now have plenty of clay to form a strong rim. If not, the process can be repeated. Don't despair if this defeats you at first, it's worth persevering with.

This basic movement of pulling up is repeated with knuckle or finger tips until the walls are sufficiently thin in proportion to the size of the pot. You will probably need to relax finger pressure slightly as you near the top of the pot. A cut section will tell you this. After the first pull, if unable to link left thumb with right knuckle, use your thumbs to link your hands together, unless the pot is too big. When you have graduated to bigger pots you will have sufficient strength of arm to hold your hands firmly without linking them. Incidentally, no hand positions are obligatory, you may well find more efficient and comfortable methods of using hands and fingers than are suggested here.

Learn first to make cylinders. The impulse of clay on the wheel is to flare outward with the centrifugal force; learn to control this before going on to make open shapes.

Before making a bowl think of its shape. A cylinder has a flat base and the wall and right angles to it. A bowl has a rounded base that continues the same shape up the wall; therefore, when you open out the clay you will need this round shape. When pulling up the wall, do not open it out too quickly, pull up straight until the wall is fairly thin, then make the last shaping. If you open out the shape too soon, it will collapse. To open out the clay, apply pressure from the inner fingers and support the wall from the outside. Move your hands in a steady, even curve.

You will undoubtedly want to keep your first pot—but really you should cut it in half to see exactly how well you have done. Draw the wire halfway under the pot, then quickly up, slicing it neatly in half. Study the section—it should be of even thickness across the bottom and up the sides.

A common fault—and a bad one—is an uneven base. A bumpy base will throw the pot off center and the walls will not be even. If you have this trouble, work at leveling the base after the opening-out stage: Your thumb may not be strong enough yet to flatten the clay in one movement, so use the tips of your fingers for this leveling, work inwards to the center and remember to steady the rest of the pot.

A newly thrown pot, cut in half to examine the thickness of walls and bottom.

Cutting off a weak or uneven rim and removing the clay.

Another common fault is thickness at the bottom of the wall. In the future, make the first pull up with both hands —one inside the pot and one outside—grasping the whole wall of the pot. This is also necessary when working a large amount of clay.

If the completed pot has one side higher than the other it shows that you are not getting the clay properly centered before opening out. But you can recenter the clay *after* opening out. Again, use both hands together, grasp the clay firmly and allow it to run through your hands, controlling it with an even pressure.

When clay weakens on the wheel it is known as "tired" and a collapsed pot will "squat." This squatting can take place after the pot is removed from the wheel, but proves it was pretty weak anyway. You need to learn how far you can take clay, and the "feel" clay has just before it collapses, so keep throwing until this happens. If the top of the pot starts to cave in, then cut the weak part off and continue throwing with what clay remains. To "cut off," have the wheel running and the left hand poised above the part to be cut. Use a needle to cut gradually through the pot below the weak part, catch the cut ring quickly and lift it away as it separates from the body of the pot. Then steady the rim as before. Alternately, use a short wire and, with the wheel running, cut down from the top of the pot until you reach the stronger area. Hold the wire steady a moment. Then lift wire and cut piece of clay up and away.

If the clay flares out and you can't control it with the normal pulling movement, use both hands linked at the thumbs with fingers spread round the outside of the pot. Start at the bottom, or you will throw the pot off center, but do not apply pressure until you have reached the part of the pot you want to bring in. This movement is called "collaring" and is used to make the narrow neck of a bottle. Throw and collar alternately to keep the wall even. When the hole is too narrow to insert even a finger, use a round, slurry-coated stick. Watch that you do not trap a pool of slurry inside the pot— particularly when making a closed shape—use a sponge attached to a long stick to absorb any moisture left inside. Only use a sponge when the wheel is running, never dab at a stationary pot. However, don't run the wheel unless working, this weakens the pot unnecessarily.

Avoid running out of clay for the rim by relaxing finger pressure as you near the top of the pot. Experiment with forming different rims with fingers and thumb and always smooth over the finished surface with a chamois leather or sponge.

At intervals when forming a pot, stand a bit away from the wheel and look at it from all angles. Always looking from above can be misleading.

When you think you have finished throwing, test the thickness of the base of the wall by gently inserting the cutting needle until you see the tip emerge inside the pot and mark where it entered with your thumb nail. Now you can see exactly how thick the wall is and ask yourself whether to have one more throw—the answer will probably be yes. When you

Collaring, or bringing in the top of the pot to form the narrow neck of a bottle.

Final bringing in and shaping of the pot. (Left and below)

feel any further work will do more harm than good, trim the base of the pot with a turning tool, using the point downward and cutting toward the wheelhead. If the pot starts to wobble, stop turning, you are cutting too far. Be careful not to build up a mass of clay on the tool, remove it as you go along. Right at the base of the pot cut a final indentation under the edge. Now stop the wheel. To cut the pot off the wheelhead hold the wire quite taut between your fingers and run it across the surface of the wheelhead and under the pot. To lift the pot from the wheelhead, first dry your hands and place a bat on a conveniently near flat surface. Use both hands, apply a gentle even pressure to the pot, pick it up from the wheelhead, and place it on the bat as smoothly and quickly as possible.

If the shape is a flat or open one, or you lack confidence in lifting, run slurry or water under the pot using the wire to cut through several times until the pot starts to move, then

Trimming the base of a pot with a turning tool—remember to use it with the point downward cutting toward the wheelhead.

slide it off with your fingertips onto a previously dampened bat. Any distortion should be straightened out when the pot has dried to leather-hard; an attempt to do so now would only make a mess.

A better way to cut pots off the wheelhead is to do so with the wheel running slowly—and it will give an attractive shell pattern if a twisted wire is used. This method is less alarming and a lot easier than it sounds, but don't try it with nylon wire or there will be a tendency for the pot to jump. The secret is to turn the wheel off immediately the cut is completed, but if the controls are hand-operated, this may be difficult to do.

When the pot has dried sufficiently to be handled, remove it from the bat and turn it upside down on a clean, smooth surface to ensure even drying. Pots of the same size can be placed rim to rim on top of each other, when they are leather-hard, to finish drying. Scrape bats clean or wash after use—a dirty bat will spoil the base of the next pot.

Repetition Throwing

Throwing several pots the same shape and size is called repetition throwing and is a matter of constant practice. You can keep measuring, but it is better to try to judge the pots by eye and "feel"—you will learn quicker. In theory the same amount of clay and the same hand movements will produce the same shape, but it is incredible how many variations on an original theme one can produce: members of the same family, but how distantly related?

To make a marker to help judge the size, take a thin stick and tie a strong rubber band around one end of it. Set the other end of the stick in a lump of clay near the wheelhead so that the rubber band will just touch the rim of the first pot—when the rim of the next pot comes to this point you will have reached the right size.

Personally I would be happier to see six freely thrown and lively bowls than six bowls that have been measured, struggled with and remeasured in an attempt to get exactly the same shape and size. The time spent measuring could be better spent practicing to throw by eye, for this is the only way to become proficient in repetition throwing—practice, practice,

practice. However, if you want to measure, use the calipers and remember to write down the measurements of the shape you are throwing, in case you reset the calipers before making this shape again.

Throwing on Bats

However carefully you lift or slide pots from the wheelhead there is always the possibility of the shape being distorted or even collapsing altogether. A bent rim can be tapped straight when leather-hard, but collapsed pots can't be made as good as new—only into something else. Many potters prefer to throw on bats and remove each piece together with its bat from the wheel, enabling them to throw the next immediately.

To fix a bat to the wheelhead, place rolls of fairly damp clay on the wheelhead, and then tap the bat onto the clay, making sure it is centered. Run the wheel slowly and use your fist to tap it down as it rotates until it is running true. The dampness of the clay will ensure adhesion, but it will be simple to lift the bat off by inserting the tip of a knife between bat and clay—or just cut through the supporting clay with the wire. This is especially useful for bigger pots or flat shapes which otherwise need to dry a bit before being taken from the wheel.

Notes on Throwing Big Pots

It will be some time before you are tackling weights of 10 pounds and over on the wheel; there is no virtue in learning to control a large amount of clay in the early stages and then throwing a medium-sized, clumsy pot with it. Gradually increase the amount of clay used and make sure that the pots grow correspondingly bigger.

When preparing balls of clay for bigger pots, it is easier to roll them into shape on the table. For weights of 8 pounds and over don't try to get a ball shape, start with a cone and beat it onto the wheelhead with your hands, using a slow wheel. This will assist the business of centering, but don't start with the clay too flat.

Use a much slower wheel for centering and coning and take your time. The condition of the clay is even more important; take special care with wedging. Make quite sure that the clay is running really true before opening out—any faults will be that much harder to correct with a large mass of clay. Linking the fingers of both hands will make coning easier. For making the hole, use not just your thumb, but the whole hand, formed into a tight fist. Making a slight depression with both thumbs will give a good start. When you have opened out the pot use the fingers of the right hand, supported by the left hand, to smooth the bottom. Then make sure that it is still on center by using both hands firmly to squeeze the ring of clay as it runs through them. This may leave a bulge of clay on the edge of the inside—if so, it should be worked in

Open out a large bowl by using the right wrist steadied by the left hand.

Smoothing the bottom of a big bowl. (Above) Recenter a large bowl
by using both hands to firmly squeeze the ring of clay as it runs
through them. (Below)

toward the center of the bottom and, if necessary, lifted off with a finger.

The first pull up can be made using both hands held together at the wrist from the *outside* of the pot and "lifting" the clay up, or use one hand inside and one hand outside, linked with both thumbs at the top.

For large, flat plates or bowls, open out the clay using the base of the right hand pushing from the wrist and steadied by the left hand. The floor of the pot can be made smooth with a rubber kidney or a tool made from wood or plastic.

If you are not satisfied with a big pot but feel it will collapse if you continue to work on it, leave it dry out for a few hours to firm the top few inches—you will still be able to throw. It is generally the bottom that requires more clay lifted up, but you can still dampen the upper part of the pot with a sponge if it has dried too much. However, it is necessary to leave more clay at the base of the wall to support the weight of a bigger pot. It's a good idea to finish the rim when the wall has hardened somewhat; you will be able to apply more pressure and get a better finish.

The first pull up of a large bowl.

TURNING AND ITS USES

"Turning" or "trimming" are names for the process of cutting away surplus clay from a heavy base or making a footring. Turn on a kick wheel if possible; you have more control and can vary the speed of the wheel more easily.

Make sure turning tools are always kept sharp and clean —they won't do the job if they are blunt or dirty. Keep tools for turning leather-hard pots separate from those you use to cut the surplus clay from freshly thrown pots; for this work use a piece of wood cut to the right shape instead of a metal tool, which will soon become blunted.

Before starting to turn, remember that the outer shape of the pot should correspond to the inner shape—any surplus clay should be cut away. When a footring is cut from a bowl, the finished bowl should look as if the ring had been *added* to the original shape.

A well-thrown pot should not need to be turned; a knife or wooden tool can be used to tidy the bottom edge, and sponge and finger used to smooth it. However, a wet pot can be deceptive and when leather-hard may reveal a thick base that spoils the whole shape. Bowls do not necessarily need a footring, but certain shapes show to better advantage with the "lift" that a foot gives.

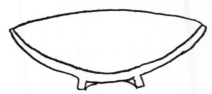

Section of a bowl with footring.

How to Turn

Place the leather-hard pot upside down in the center of the wheelhead. Check that it is exactly on center by running the wheel slowly and bringing a pencil or needle slowly in to come into contact with the pot, where you intend to cut clay away. The marks made will show if you need to move the pot, and in which direction. Beginners' pots are often not true at the rim *and* base—try to turn an off-center pot and you run the risk of cutting through one side of it. Make sure you have the part of the pot to be turned quite true before securing it on the wheelhead. To do this, hold the pot with the left hand and secure it with rolls of clay pressed down to the *wheelhead*. The clay must support the rim of the pot but not press into it, or the shape will be spoiled, and a distorted pot is difficult to turn. Now run the wheel fairly fast, steady your arms as for throwing, and hold the turning tool with both hands. Resting one finger along the top of the pot while you work will give you warning if it starts to jump. Bring the sharp edge of the tool gently into contact with the part of the pot to be cut away. When the pot is exactly right for turning—not too damp or too dry—the clay will come away in easy, smooth corkscrews or curls—known as "turnings." If the base has an uneven edge, or if there is a "bump" on the bottom or side of the pot, stop the wheel and scrape it away with a metal kidney. The tool will tend to jump on any unevenness. For the same reason, fill in any dents or holes with leather-hard clay.

To turn a footring on a bowl: First use the sharp point of the tool to mark the outer ring of the foot (1), then cut in toward the first cut at right angles from the outside (2). Next tackle the outer wall of the bowl, leaving the inner part of the ring until last. Use the sharp point of the tool again to cut down, marking the inside of the footring (3) before removing the rest of the clay with the side or heel of the tool. Stop the wheel at intervals and tap the pot with the tip of your finger—when you feel a slight "spring" in response to pressure, you have cut far enough. When you have finished turning, avoid a harsh edge by running your finger or a sponge over the turned section.

If your efforts result in an uneven pattern instead of a smooth surface, either the tool is blunt, the pot too dry, or both. This pattern is known as "chattering." It has possibilities for decoration, but not around the thick base of a pot. If you know the tool is sharp, then dampen the pot by running a moist sponge over the part to be turned while the wheel is in motion—but watch that the drips don't run down to the rim or into the supporting clay. Use the sharp point of the tool to cut through the chattering, then use the side of the tool to cut it away. If a pot is too dry and sponging is not drastic enough, remove it from the wheelhead and dip it quickly into water. Then put the pot on a bat until the water has been absorbed and repeat until it is damp enough.

If, however, the clay is too damp, the tool will tend to catch and the pot may jump out of the protective rolls of clay. Don't attempt to work under these conditions, set the pot aside until it is really leather-hard.

Some potters prefer to turn on a pad of leather-hard clay.

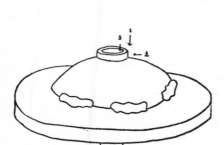

Turning a bowl.

Beat a piece of leather-hard clay flat onto the wheelhead, cut it to a circle and turn the top until it is quite flat. Now make a shallow indentation in which to set the pot. Supporting rolls of clay will still be necessary and, if you are turning several pots in succession, you must "tidy up" the pad, removing all turnings to avoid marking the rim of the next pot. For bowls, a dome of leather-hard clay can be shaped as a support. If this is high enough, the rim will not touch the wheelhead and the bowl can be held in place with pads of clay *underneath* between the support and the inner surface of the bowl.

If a pot is distorted, tap it gently back into shape with your fingers, but don't force it. If the rim is cracked or chipped, it is seldom worth the trouble of patching, and it is generally simpler to make another pot. However, if you really want to save a precious piece whose rim has been cracked by careless handling, break out a rough triangle at the point of the crack. Score the edges of pot and broken piece, apply slurry and fit the two parts carefully together. Allow very slow drying and give the section a final tidying before the clay is too dry. The rough edges caused by the break will join more readily than a cut surface.

Awkward shapes such as bottles or narrow-necked pieces can either be turned right way up or set neck down in a "chuck." A chuck is a shape that supports work for turning. A thick thrown shape dried to leather-hard is most efficient. Chucks can be kept in a damp cupboard (see page 143) or cookie tin, but need to be watched as they may dry out over a period of time. The best shape for a chuck is one that flares outward slightly so that most shapes and sizes can be accommodated. Center and support the chuck as you would a pot, then fit the pot to be turned into it and support this too.

Alternatively, throw a chuck at the same time as the pot. You will then be able to make exactly the right shape for this particular piece. The mouth of the chuck can be turned with a tool when leather-hard to alter its shape if necessary. If the chuck is on the moist side, line it with tissue or soft paper to prevent the pot sticking inside. When you have finished turning you can scrape away the turnings, damp the chuck down and rethrow it into a pot in its own right, or else keep it for future use as a chuck.

Another pot can be set up on the wheelhead as a chuck, but without the natural adhesion of clay to clay you will need

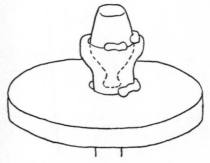

Pot held in chuck for turning.

74

to support both pots carefully. To turn large flat plates too large to fit on top of the wheelhead, pad the edge of the wheelhead with a thin roll of clay, sit the plate carefully over this, and secure it with pads of clay underneath.

Notes on Assembly

Before making any pots composed of several parts, remember that base, lid, knob, etc. must be thrown from the same batch of wedged clay, otherwise different water content (or different body) may cause varying rates of shrinkage.

When assembling such a pot it is essential that all parts have the same water content. Any pieces that have dried too rapidly can be moistened by rapid immersion in water. But be sure that all moisture is absorbed before putting the pot down, or puddles will form and the piece will rapidly degenerate into slip. A sponge can be used for damping pieces, but it is harder to apply an even amount of moisture this way. A really dry pot can be damped down by wrapping it in a wrung-out wet cloth, covering the whole in a layer of plastic and leaving it for a few days. However, do not leave it too long without checking, the pot will eventually become so wet as to lose its shape.

You only learn how much water clay holds when you try to replace it in a dry pot.

When assembling, keep hands, pot, and work surface as clean as possible. Clear up little bits of clay before they attach themselves to the nearest surface and keep a damp sponge and a dry towel close at hand. Pots can be tidied up with a damp sponge, but the more sponging the less "life" the pot will have, so try to handle work as little as possible. You will need a supply of thick slip, a tool for scoring and a wooden tool for reaching those parts where your finger won't go.

Handles

Pulling handles is difficult, and requires much practice to do it well. Handles need to be strong but not clumsy, and the most graceful handles are formed by "pulling." Make sure the clay is thoroughly wedged for this, and slightly stiffer than for throwing. Have your pot in front of you and consider carefully the size and shape of handle needed and where you are going to place it.

Use about half a pound of wedged clay and beat it out into a long, thin cube by slapping it down on the table first on one side and then on the other, turning it all the time. Holding the cube in your left hand, moisten your right hand and pull the end of the cube down between finger and thumb, stretching and thinning the clay. Repeat this movement, turning the handle as you pull it and making sure you pull it straight—a crookedly pulled handle will twist back in the firing to its original shape, even if you straighten it when applying it to the pot.

If you feel any weakness or impurity in the clay, break it off at that point and start again. Work until the handle is as thin as you need, but still has "spring" and life. Now break off the length you have pulled and attach the thicker end to a bat, letting the other end fall into a natural curve. Leave the handle to harden slightly before fixing it to the pot.

Learn to pull small handles first before attempting large ones, and practice before you have a pot that needs a handle. Even when you have mastered the first principles and are ready to put a handle on a pot, be sure to pull several—you may spoil your first attempts.

Handles dry very fast and can be pulled after the rest of the pot has been made—before you start turning is a good time. They will dry out surprisingly quickly in a warm place, so keep an eye on them; although handles can be quickly dipped in water to dampen them, it is obviously better to avoid this.

To fix to the pot, the handle needs to be stiff enough to hold its shape, but supple enough to stand the pressure you will apply to its ends as you attach it. It may be necessary to dampen the ends, as they tend to dry out more quickly. Trim both ends straight, score the leather-hard pot, apply a dab of slip to the handle or to the pot, and press the top section gently into place, supporting the inside of the pot as you do so. Work the top end of the handle well into the pot and then fasten the bottom end in the same way. Small rolls or pads of clay can be worked in if extra strength is needed. When you have fixed the handle, and tidied any surplus slip away (ideally there should be none to tidy), run a damp finger under the curve of the handle.

Pulling a handle. Hold the cube in your left hand, moisten your right hand and pull the end of the cube down between finger and thumb, stretching and thinning the clay.

A second method for pulling a handle. Hold clay in your left hand, wrap your right hand behind it, and use your thumb to pull the front in alternate strokes down each side.

Handles can be pulled from a piece of clay previously attached to the pot, but this calls for some degree of skill and is not recommended as a starting point. An easier method is to pull the handle somewhat thicker, leave it flat on a bat to dry slightly, then to fix the top end to the pot. Give the handle a few more pulls with a wet hand to give it a good shape, then hold the bottom end and jerk it slightly so that the handle forms a loop. Finally, fasten the bottom end of the handle to the pot. Here the danger is that the handle may become too damp and spring away from the pot as the pot dries, so be particularly careful to dry the whole slowly.

A different method of pulling handles is to take a very

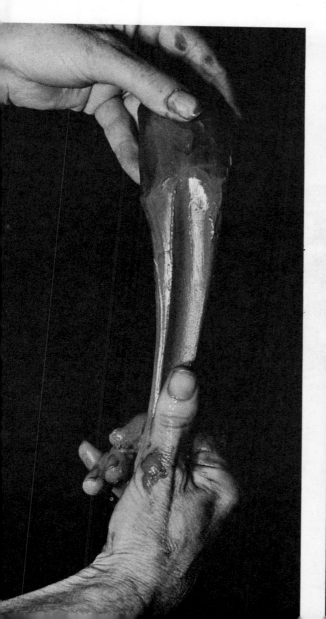
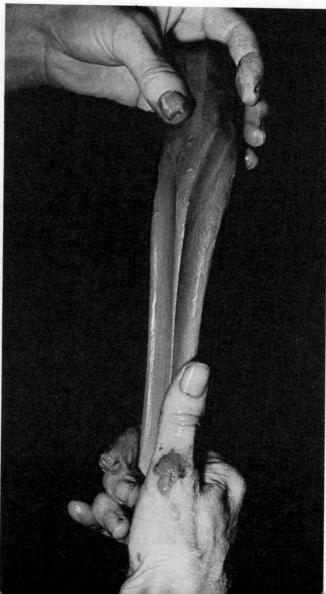

much larger roll of clay—well wedged, of course, but softer. Wrap your right hand behind it—your left hand will hold the clay as before—and use your thumb to pull the front in alternate strokes down each side while your fingers shape the back. This is a better way of pulling larger handles, they will be stronger.

A thumb stop on the handle makes a big pot easier to hold when pouring out or drinking from it. This is just a roll of clay attached at the top of the handle after it has been fixed to the pot.

For large teapots or jugs, an extra handle can be fitted so that the pot is lifted with both hands.

Handles can also be rolled, but this is clumsy for mugs, jugs, etc. Cane handles are very graceful on teapots; to house a cane handle, two small loops are pulled or rolled and fixed to the pot. Teapots can also be made with an "overhead" handle made with a half-circle strip cut from a thrown pot. This is

Thrown pitcher set by Vally Possony. (Photo by Claire Flanders.)

also a good idea for the side handles of casseroles—they can be cut from a small thrown bowl.

A thrown cone shape can also be used as a handle, or a thrown piece cut in half. However, too heavy a handle will cause the pot to distort in the firing.

A deep footring turned on a casserole lid will make a good handle, having the advantage that, being one with the lid, it is unlikely to be knocked off—always a risk with an added handle. The lid can also double as a plate.

Always cover any pot with a handle, spout, or added knob or leave it to dry very slowly. If dried in a warm atmosphere, any addition will dry more quickly than the pot and pull away as the clay shrinks in drying. Plastic sheets or bags are excellent for keeping the pot covered until drying is well under way.

If the joining process is hindered by the clay being too stiff at any point, dampen the parts and wait until they are soft enough. If handles "spring" off when the pot is dry, you

A variety of types of handles.

are probably fixing them on before they have dried sufficiently; i.e., when they are much wetter than the pots. Or maybe you are not applying them firmly. Or drying them too fast.

Saucers

Some people find saucers an unnecessary fuss and simply drink from mugs. However, if you have good furniture or can't bear to see your guests worry about what to do with the spoon, saucers are necessary. To be efficient, the cup or mug should fit into a shallow indentation, the saucer should hold a spoon comfortably and be easy to pick up. No saucer should be designed without its cup and vice versa. A wide-based cup or mug will need a wide indentation in the saucer, and you still need room for the spoon—this can make the saucer somewhat large and clumsy.

The basic method of making saucers is to throw a shallow bowl with a thick base. Use a piece of wood or finger tip to make the indentation and be sure that it is quite flat, or the cup will wobble. If you like a footring, turn this at the thickest part of the base—just outside the indentation area. It is helpful to have calipers set up for measuring cups and saucers. The leather-hard measurement of the base of the cup, indentation ring, and *inner* ring of foot should all be the same.

Section of saucer with footring.

Lips

The simplest lip is pulled on the jug immediately after taking it off the wheel, while it is freshly thrown. It will help you to learn how to do this if you run your fingers over a fired jug that has a lip that you like.

The pot will need a firm, strong rim. With damp hands, support the rim with forefinger and thumb of the left hand an inch or two apart—according to the size of the intended lip —and, with the forefinger or little finger of the right hand gently rub the clay so held from side to side, stretching and bending it down to form a lip. Start forming the pouring channel well down the neck of the pot—it will be more efficient. Be careful not to split the clay where the spout is stretched; this can be patched at the leather-hard stage, but spontaneity will be lost. Thrown pots can also be cut up to make lips.

Making a simple lip on a freshly thrown jug. (Right)

80

Pot made from thrown shapes.

Thrown shapes pinched and modeled.

Coiled pot, burnished with iron oxide.

Coiled pot, dripped glaze.

The pot supported by sticks for glaze pouring.

Glazing the inside of a bowl by pouring the glaze in and rotating the bowl as the glaze is poured out.

Pouring glaze over the outside of the bowl.

Different Glaze Techniques: Unglazed vase.   *Double dipping.*

Glazed with color and another color poured over.

Iron oxide brushed on with a painter's brush.   *Iron oxide brushed on a rotating pot.*

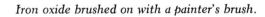

Textures imprinted on leather-hard clay with screws, modeling tools, drinking straws, etc.

Glaze alters the outline and effect of these textures. (Below)

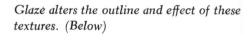

Spouts

Spouts are thrown in a cone shape and cut off to fit the pot when leather-hard. To throw a spout, push your thumb right to the wheelhead when making the hole, and open out so that the spout has no base—the bottom of the spout should be wide enough to fit well over the teapot, and then shaped into the pouring end.

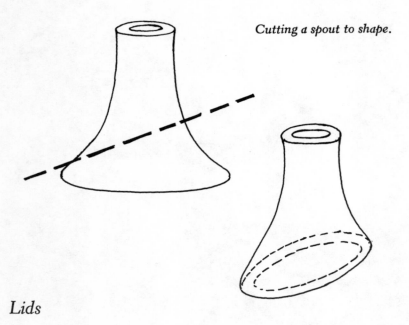

Cutting a spout to shape.

Lids

Lids can be made in a variety of ways from different wheel-thrown shapes. Not all lids need a gallery to rest on; they can be made to fit into the neck of the pot, or simply to rest on top of it. Support can also be provided by a flange on the lid.

Unless making a small pot, forming the gallery on a thrown pot is best done before the walls are completed, while they are still strong enough to take downward pressure without distorting. A sufficient amount of clay must be brought up to the rim to enable a strong, firm gallery to be made. And need I add that the pot must be quite true? Most of the work is done with the left hand: left thumb to steady the outside of the rim; left forefinger to form the gallery; left middle finger to support the inside; right forefinger rests on the left thumb

Making a gallery for a lid to rest on. Most of the work is done by the left hand.

to steady the top of the rim. Bring both hands gently into position on the slow-running pot and carefully press your left forefinger down until you have formed a sufficiently deep gallery. All the time you will need to support the other points of contact. If the whole thing runs away with you, best cut it off and start again. The end of a stick, well dipped in slurry, will do the job of pressing down the gallery if you decide your fingers are simply the wrong shape. But, again, support all round as you go.

A gallery can also be made on the outside of the pot, so that the line of pot and lid are one. However, there is little room for error with this kind of lid and you must measure very carefully. To make the gallery use your left hand to support the rim and your right forefinger to form the gallery. Again, you may find it easier to use the edge of a stick or ruler. Now you can return to thinning the wall of the pot, but always steady the gallery at the end of a throw. Measure the gallery carefully before removing the pot from the wheel.

Now to the different kinds of lid. The simplest is thrown flat on the wheelhead with its knob in place. After the clay is centered and coned, leave enough clay in the middle of the ball for the knob, and press down each side of this with forefingers and thumbs. Then work the clay down from the center to the edge of the lid until it is thin enough, measuring to see if the size is right. The thickness of the lid should be the same as that of the wall of the pot, but if the lid is domed slightly toward the knob the shape of pot and lid will be more pleasing. Having thrown the rest of the lid, return to the knob and throw this into whatever shape you wish, using your fingertips. If you make the lid too big, hold the calipers over the moving pot and gently bring one arm down until it just marks the clay. When a complete circle is marked on the clay you will have the correct measurement to fit the gallery. Cut away any surplus clay and finish the lid with an undercut. This will make the lid "sit" better and help in removing it from the wheelhead. Finally, run a damp sponge over the rim. If you cut this kind of lid through and immediately lift it by the knob, it should come off the wheelhead. However, if it doesn't, resort to wire and slurry to slide it off. This lid is illustrated on the middle pot in the back row and on the left-hand pot in the front row.

The second and third types of lid illustrated are thrown

upside down. The simpler type (back row, left) is made like a deep bowl with slides sloping inwards, so that the lid will fit into the neck of the pot. The other (front row, right) is made like a conventional teapot lid, with a flange to fit into a gallery or rest on top of the pot. This lid is easily thrown: when opening out, press the third finger of the left hand down on the clay, about one-quarter to one-half inch from the edge—which will still be controlled by the little finger. This will form the ridge for the flange. You can then thin the inner wall that fits inside the pot.

When leather-hard, the top is turned and a knob (either thrown or modeled) or a pulled handle is stuck on if desired. However, this is not always necessary: A lid fitting into a gallery needs a knob to lift it by, but if it fits over the rim of the pot it can be just as easy to lift without one. Knobs can be thrown separately and added to the lid while the top is being turned. Alternatively, a knob or footring can be turned out of the top of the lid—but you must leave plenty of clay at the base when throwing. A footring will serve as a practical handle to a casserole lid and enable it to double as a plate. This is shown on the right-hand pot in the front row. To make a knob really one with the lid, a small piece of clay can be stuck straight onto a newly turned lid, dampened and thrown into shape. The secret of success is to use the minimum of slurry and to make sure the base of the lid and supporting clay do not become moist.

The fourth lid (back row, right) is also thrown upside down, but without the sharp angle to fit into the gallery or over the rim of the pot. The angle of this lid is designed to fit into the angle of the opening of the pot. This is easy to make as it allows some margin for error of measurement. The top is turned as for the previous two types, and again can have knob, handle, or be left plain.

Always be very careful when measuring lid and base and make sure you are measuring the right part. A lid to fit into a gallery will need to be measured on the *outer* angle, as the whole lid will fit into the gallery. On the other hand, if the lid is designed so that the flange fits *into* the pot and the edge of the lid overhangs the pot, then obviously the angle to fit *into* the inside must be measured. Rest the calipers gently on the pot when measuring, holding them crookedly in the air will give a false measurement.

Several kinds of lids. (Overleaf.)

Pots can be thrown in one with a lid, and the lid cut through at the leather-hard stage, when it should drop neatly onto the base. To do this, throw a closed shape with a knob on top. Then use a stick or the edge of a ruler to make the indentation that will become the outside gallery. When the pot is leather-hard, set it up on the wheel and cut through the top of the indentation with the needle. However, it is not all that easy to judge the shape of the lid to fit over the gallery and you may have to trim a little clay off the inside of the lid.

Additional lids made by the author.

Teapots

The teapot is considered "the pinnacle of the potter's art". A teapot that pours well, doesn't drip or let the lid crash into the teacup when being poured, and is also balanced and pleasing to look at is not easy to achieve. Put due thought into your first—and all the others, of course. Make several drawings before you decide which design to follow, and remember it is best not to be too ambitious. You obviously need container, lid, handle, and spout. But what sort of handle: A conventional handle opposite the spout, or at the side of the pot? A cane handle or a cut section of thrown pot—or a thrown handle? And which kind of lid? Do you need a gallery for the lid to sit in or not? To do without the gallery makes the pot considerably easier to make and lighter to use. Having cut out the gallery, you could then cut out the knob; it is just as easy to pick up a teapot lid by its rim as by a handle, provided the rim is not resting in a gallery. How long do you want to make the spout? Consider the angle of the pot that the base of the spout will have to fit over and work out the width needed. Remember, the top of the spout will mark the height of liquid the pot will hold. Fit the spout too low and water will pour out onto the table as you proudly serve your first cup of tea. Too narrow a spout will pour slowly. Too wide a spout will pour too fast and splash. The design of the spout is very important: a teapot or jug stands or falls by its pouring performance. A spout thrown in a straight continuous line with a smooth inner surface (i.e., no throwing ridges) will pour better than a dumpy rounded shape. Incidentally, some potters find that their spouts tend to twist, to "unwind," in the firing, and have to put them on slightly crooked in the first place to compensate for this. This is likely to be caused by the composition of the clay body.

Consider the size of the parts in relation to the whole—you will be surprised how the addition of the handle will alter your view of the spout.

Making a Teapot

First throw the pot part of the teapot. To be on the safe side, throw at least two lids and several spouts of different

shapes and sizes. The shape you planned on paper may not, in fact, look so good on the pot after all. You may prefer another. Spouts dry more quickly than lids or bases, so either throw them later or protect them from rapid drying. When all parts are hard, turn the base if necessary. Next finish the lid —you will be able to judge the positions for the spout and handle more easily with the lid in place.

Cut any surplus clay from *inside* the base of your chosen spout and shape it so that it will sit easily on the teapot base, testing it constantly against the base and being careful not to cut too much away. You may need to press the spout gently into shape so that it will fit snugly. Now hold the spout in the place you are going to fix it and mark round the outline. This will give the area in which you will cut the holes to catch the tea leaves. Do this with a special piercing tool and be careful to get all the loose bits of clay out of the pot afterward with a spoon. Cut enough holes to ensure the area cut out is as great as the area of the spout opening. This aids pouring. Score over the marking, smear a thin layer of slip along the area scored and press the spout gently into place, supporting the pot from inside as you do so. If necessary,

A traditional teapot and jug by the author. This teapot has a gallery for the lid to sit on and thrown handles on the lid and pot.

A pleasingly shaped porcelain teapot by Nan Rothwell with handleless lid. (Photo by Cynthia Brumback.)

smooth a very thin roll of clay over the join. Any roughness or unevenness where spout and pot meet can be removed with a fine hacksaw blade and then smoothed over. The spout should seem to grow out of the base, not look as if it had been added as an afterthought. If you prefer it, the top of the spout can be cut off at the conventional angle, or the thrown end left untouched. Some people think a pot pours better if the spout is cut off. This is done with the determined stroke of a wet knife and the edges sponged smooth.

The handle is added last, and the whole pot protected from too rapid drying.

While assembling any pot, look at it from all angles. Make sure handles, spouts, etc. are straight and in the right place.

And a coffee pot: It is really a thin teapot with a large hole at the base of the spout instead of several smaller ones.

Composite pots

Big pots can be made in sections. Two bowls can be thrown and joined to make a fat pot, two or more cylinders thrown and joined for a tall pot. Measurements must be carefully made and the edges to be joined be strong enough to unite without cracking. When throwing the parts remember the angle at which they will join and shape the rim accordingly. Two cylinders will be joined on two flat rims, but a cylinder used as a base for a bowl will need a sloping rim to join the curve of the bowl.

The usual advice on all assembly work applies, but you are not so bound by practical considerations as when making tableware and will have far more scope with design. If possible, join the sections so that the join fits in with the design of the pot, rather than attempt a perfectly smooth join on the side of the wall. The slightest flaw will show when the pot has been fired and fine cracks (or large drastic ones) may appear. One way round this difficulty is to give the pot a rough texture or scratched surface so that any hair cracks will be camouflaged.

If you decide the shape is too weak in any place, clay can be smoothed on after you have assembled the work. Big pots offer great scope for texturing and bold decoration.

Figures and abstract shapes can also be made out of thrown sections. But remember there will be a risk of a tall

An unusual candelabrum, 2 feet high, made by Ruth Duckworth, using techniques similar to those for composite pots. (Courtesy, American Crafts Council.)

figure bending over in the firing and becoming stuck in the glaze of the next pot (or, horrors, the kiln wall). Pads of clay can be used as supports and dried and fired with the figure. However, when you get to the glaze firing (and the higher the firing, the greater the risk of a figure bending) remember not to glaze the parts where the props meet the figure.

Decorative Plaques

Ceramic plaques or wall tiles give plenty of scope for texture and color. It is wise to use an open body, the better to withstand the unusual stresses of varying thickness. Start with a large, thick slab of clay and you will have depth for making textures without risk of the plaque cracking. Large thick sheets of clay are far less likely to buckle than thin ones, but you can also take the precaution of scoring the back of the plaque with shallow cuts at regular intervals. This should be done at the leather-hard stage. Remember to make holes in the piece to hang it up by.

Thrown pots, either whole or in sections, can form part of the design, and areas of glass will add color and depth. Crushed or broken glass is added after the pot has been glazed, and precautions must be taken in the original design so that the glass will not run over the edge of the plaque in the firing. White or colored glass, such as wine bottles, marbles, window-panes, can be used. When the piece cools the glass will craze in depth and give an attractive crystalline effect. Be careful not to put too much glass in too small an area—the stress of a thick pool of glass cooling within the body will cause the piece to crack. Try using plain or colored glass over glazes that contain oxides.

To break up glass bottles or large pieces, put them in separate polythene bags and give them a good bang with a hammer (not another bottle, the second bottle may shatter and cut your hand, leaving the bottle you attacked intact on the ground). Obviously pieces of glass should be kept under control and not allowed to get into clay or glazes.

Glass cannot be used to decorate functional pieces because of the chance of splinters working loose; nor can it decorate perpendicular work, because it runs far and fast, but it is fine for ash trays or decorative plates.

An interesting large piece of relief tile, titled "Innocent City" by the artist, Kenneth Dierck, and composed of many smaller tiles. (Courtesy, American Crafts Council.)

DECORATION AND TEXTURES

Here are some ideas for methods of decoration; but "decoration" is a bad word, implying something applied or added to make the original catch the eye. A good pot does not need gimmicks; slip, brushwork, texture, or glaze should not appear to have been added, but should have been conceived as part of the whole. To use a pot as a form on which to paint patterns is to debase the pot. Clay is too versatile a material to be used instead of paper, and any design should be planned with

A collection of slab-built bottles by Claude Conover. The artist has achieved a variety of surface textures by scratching with any number of tools on the leather-hard bottle or by rolling on patterns using various handmade rollers. (Courtesy, American Crafts Council.)

the shape and not be an obvious afterthought. It is easy to get carried away with the sheer pleasure of scratching, cutting, texturing, or molding, and the result of too much self-indulgence may well be a pot that gives less pleasure to the eye of the beholder than it did to the hand of the potter.

Most designs and textures are done when the work is leather-hard, but pots straight from the wheel can be bent or marked with a wet finger or hand. You can make an impression, trail a design, or make a series of indentations. A pattern of impressions can be made by slapping a wooden tool or piece of bamboo against a pot as soon as it is dry enough to handle.

The shape and pattern made by turnings as they fall will give you ideas. A leather-hard pot can be painted over with slurry and quickly rolled onto a bed of fresh turnings. You may need to press the larger pieces into place, or if you aim for a random effect, be prepared to lose some of the turnings when the pot dries and they drop off.

A more formal design can be scratched on the leather-hard clay, using a variety of tools. For a repeat design you can make a special roller. Make a thick ring of clay with a small hole in the center (big enough to allow strong wire to be threaded through). When leather-hard, cut a pattern on the outer rim of this ring. After biscuit firing, thread a piece of wire through the hole and twist the ends of the wire together to make a handle.

For an all-over texture, string, rope, or rough-textured material can be wrapped firmly round a leather-hard pot. Remove this before firing or you'll get smoke from the kiln.

When a body with a high grog content is allowed to dry and then scraped with a metal kidney or sandpaper, an interesting texture will result. Grog can be pressed in while the clay is still fairly damp for this effect if you don't want to work with a rough textured clay.

Pots can be thrown with a deliberately thick wall and slices of clay cut out, or deep incisions made with a potato peeler or similar tool. If you want a really rough, nubbly surface, comb the clay with a coarse hack saw blade or saw while it is still fairly damp. Then sponge the rough pieces that have been dragged by the teeth of the tool to make sure they stay in place. Extra dabs of clay can be added by hand to give an even more varied surface.

Assorted lamp bases by Nancy Wickham Boyd which have been
decorated by scratching techniques. (Photo by Hans van Nes,
courtesy, American Crafts Council.)

The field of texture is endless and you will soon have many ideas. Even the tops of pens, screws, nails—all can combine to make interesting decoration. The bark of trees will give beautiful impressions, and slabs of clay can be pressed round the tree before being dried out sufficiently to be assembled. This is a bit tricky though, so start with small pieces. Rice can be scattered over a soft surface and pressed in; it will fire away in the kiln leaving a random design. When making textured slabbed pots, texture the slabs before assembling the pot—you may have to touch up a bit where the joins come, but it will be much easier. Rolling out slabs of clay on different kinds of cloth will give many different textures. Use the cloth as much as possible when you handle the slabs so as not to spoil the texture.

On this flower vase, John J. O'Leary used a raised decoration to create the effect desired. (Courtesy, American Crafts Council.) (Right)

Craftsman John J. O'Leary gave this open-dish casserole a primitive Indian feeling through the use of heavy carved decoration. (Courtesy, American Crafts Council.)

Slipware

Slip is a very versatile form of decoration, usually associ-
ated with earthenware, but also interesting to use for stoneware. Slip is a mixture of 50 per cent clay and 50 per cent
water to which coloring matter in the form of oxides can be
added. It is easy to control and apply, but cracking will occur
if the clay of the body and of the slip have different rates of
contraction and so pull away from each other in the drying.
However, this fault can be put right by the addition of flint
to the slip, or by applying slip to the pot after it has been
bisque fired.

If the body you use is light in color, make slip by drying
out a few pounds of clay, weighing it dry and adding the percentage of oxide for the color you require (see below). Then
add water to make a thick mixture and sieve it through an
80-mesh sieve to ensure the even distribution of oxide and
eliminate lumps. It is obviously an advantage to make slip
from the same clay as the body, but if the body is dark and
you wish to make light-colored slip, this is not practical.

For a white slip, use the following recipe:

> 1 part ball clay
> 1 part China clay
> 1 part flint

Coloring (but this is just a beginning)

Gray-blue	add 1% cobalt
	2% red iron oxide
Black (use red clay base)	3% iron oxide
	2% cobalt
	2% manganese
Light gray (use white clay base)	1% iron chromate
Medium gray (use white clay base)	2% iron chromate

A list of oxides and the colors they give is on page 155.

Red slip can be made from red clay in the same way as
shown above—this will give a particularly rich color for stoneware—but the word "red" is somewhat misleading; a red slip
in earthenware fires to a tan color and in stoneware to a rich
purple-brown.

Slip is applied when the pot is leather-hard or to biscuit, and is particularly easy to apply to dishes or bowls made in plaster-of-paris molds. The support given by the mold enables you to apply more slip without fear of collapse than you could to an unsupported pot. When used alone over coarse clay without a covering of glaze, slip is known as "engobe."

An earthenware pitcher by Nan Rothwell with a clear glaze over slip. (Photo by Cynthia Brumback.)

Using Slip in Molds

Pour the slip into the dish-in-the-mold, swirl it round, and then quickly empty it out, wiping away any spilled on the rim with a sponge. Work quickly so that the pot does not absorb too much slip and lose its shape. A small amount of a different color can be poured in while the first layer is still wet, and the mold given rapid jerks and movements to cause the two slips to swirl round and merge. This is known as "marbling" and very attractive random patterns can be formed in this way.

Another method of slip decoration is to allow the first coat to harden and then to trail lines in another color across the pot. Before the lines have a chance to set, draw a feather across, pulling one line into another. This is known as "feathering." To draw the lines a slip trailer is needed. This is a small rubber syringe with a narrow mouth. The trailer is first filled with slip, then the slip squeezed slowly out. It takes some practice, so try it on a reject pot first.

Letters and patterns can be formed with a slip trailer. However, the most accurate method of "writing" is to cover the pot with a layer of slip, then scratch out the words, leaving them "written" in the color of the body below. Wax resist can also be used for this. (See page 116.)

Another method of decoration is to lay green leaves or paper cut-outs onto the leather-hard clay before pouring on slip and then removing them when the slip has set.

Slip can be poured over leather-hard pots, or the pot can be quickly dipped in slip. When using these methods take care lest the pot become saturated with water and collapse.

A safer, but much slower, method is to paint the slip on with a brush. Several coats will be needed, successive layers being applied as the pot dries. However, never apply slip to a dry pot, it will crack and fall away.

Thrown pots can be decorated with slip before being removed from the wheel. A full brush of slip run down a wet pot on the running wheel is a simple and effective method of decoration. Start at the top and work down, avoiding a pool at the bottom. If you want a thick, covering layer of slip, let the pot dry first. Either set the pot up again on the wheel proper or use a banding wheel. Try setting the pot slightly off center and running the brushful of slip up the pot.

Sgrafitto

This is the name given to the technique of scratching through a layer of slip (or glaze) to reveal the color beneath. This must be done when the slip is set but not bone dry, or it will chip. A variation of this technique is to incise a pattern on the leather-hard clay. Slip can then be brushed or poured over the entire surface and immediately wiped off with a rubber kidney. This will fill the incised pattern with slip, emphasizing the design.

A very old method of decorating slip dishes was discovered by the hard-smoking men who spat into their work and found that the tobacco ran into the slip in an insectlike pattern. You don't need to smoke or spit, just save tobacco ash, mix it with a little water and drop it into your slipware with an eyedropper.

Bowls by Harry Horlock Stringer. The rims have been sgraffitoed through iron slip under a transparent glaze.

View inside Harry Horlock Stringer's workshop. Sgraffito biscuit
before glazing. A metal spoon was used to cut the design through
the slip.

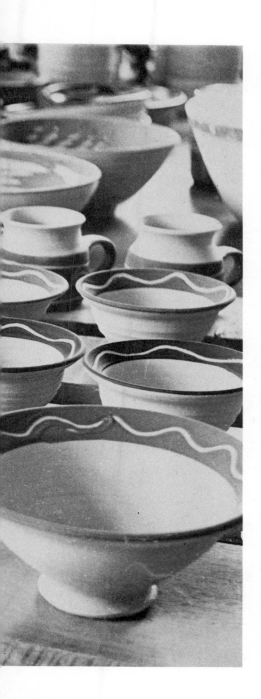

SIMPLE GLAZES

It is important to know that the most beautiful glaze can only enhance a good pot—it can't ever camouflage a bad piece of work.

The structure and composition of glazes is a fascinating and complicated subject, but if you have scant knowledge of math or chemistry, don't be put off by the pages of highly technical information in books for the advanced student. Starting with a little elementary knowledge, you will soon learn what happens, even if why and how remain a mystery for the time being. When you have gained confidence in your ability to produce glazed pots there will be plenty of time to study the subject more deeply.

Ready-made glazes can be bought from potters' merchants in many colors and textures. They are produced to conform to the highest standard, but their effect may be too flawless and "mass-produced" to satisfy you. If you want to produce more individualized work, start by buying a basic colorless glaze, and then add other ingredients to get the effect you want. The manufacturer will recommend the correct firing temperature, but remember that the addition of other materials, especially oxides, will lower the maturing temperature. If your additions make the glaze too shiny, you can add a matting agent. As a start, test small amounts of all the different glaze materials you will be using by firing them on pieces of clay or pinch pots to see how they react to the firing.

General Instructions

The following recipes for glazes have been given in parts—which can be grams, ounces, or pounds—and anyone working with only an ordinary kitchen scale will still be able to make simple glazes. But to add oxides, which are used in very small amounts, a gram scale will be necessary. However, glaze recipes are properly worked out in grams, which makes the sums much easier to calculate. Even if a glaze recipe merely says: 1 part of A, 2 parts of B, 1 part of C, use units of weight rather than of measurement and make the recipe: 25 grams A, 50 grams B, and 25 grams C. One cup of one ingredient will vary in weight from one cup of another, so that a larger batch made as the result of a successful test would give quite a different result. Like most other things, it's quicker in the end to work out the glaze formula properly, so that the final sum totals 10 or 100 parts. This will make adjusting the recipe for larger or smaller batches a simple matter.

The recipes of glazes are worked out so that the required effect; i.e., color, texture, opacity, will be obtained at a given temperature. Since all glaze ingredients melt at different temperatures, and different combinations of the same materials will melt differently, a slight adjustment of one or more of these ingredients can alter the whole character of the glaze. Obviously, glazes designed for earthenware will not be suitable to fire to stoneware temperature, and vice versa.

The ingredients to make glazes should be weighed dry and mixed in a plastic bucket or other container. Hard lumps can be ground down with a pestle and mortar, but this is not usually necessary as most materials bought from potters' merchants are in fine powder form. Water is then added, and the mixture stirred thoroughly with the hands until it is smooth enough to pass through a sieve. For fine glazes use 120-mesh, for a coarser effect use a 60-mesh sieve. A special brush can be bought to push the glaze particles through the sieve, but an ordinary nail brush will do the job as well. Don't hesitate to add more water; the thinner the mixture, the easier it will go through. It will be a simple matter to strain off the surplus liquid the next day, when the mixture has settled.

Roughly speaking, earthenware glazes should have the consistency of thin cream, while those for stoneware should be considerably thicker. However, glazes vary so much in their composition and effect that you should experiment with different thicknesses—having dipped a test piece in glaze, dip it in again, half way, so that you can judge the effect of the two thicknesses.

Earthenware Glazes

Always check with the manufacturer when buying ready-mixed earthenware glazes to make sure they do not contain lead. For centuries the principal fluxing (melting) agent used for earthenware glazes has been lead, which has long been known to be poisonous when taken orally, breathed in **vapor** form or absorbed through cuts in the skin. It has not been recognized until recently that lead can be absorbed from the glaze of a container by wine, beer, vinegar, or any other acid, and come finally to rest in whoever drinks the liquid. This is, incidentally, one theory for the decay and decline of the Roman Empire—too much wine drunk out of lead-glazed goblets resulting in mental debility. Lead is especially dangerous in that it accumulates in the body (human, this time, not the pot body); the symptoms of lead poisoning are many, and not always easily recognized.

The use of raw lead is forbidden by law in factories and workshops. To avoid the danger of poisoning, lead used in glazes is "fritted"; i.e., fired and then ground to a powder. However, even with a fritted lead glaze, no containers should be used for an acid substance. This is another argument on the side of stoneware, as lead is never used above a temperature of 2192° F. (1200° C.). At this point it vaporizes and coats the inside surface of the kiln—which doesn't do the kiln any good either.

Always take care when using fritted lead glazes: don't eat in the workshop, avoid inhaling any glaze dust, and wash your hands thoroughly after working. These precautions should also be taken when handling oxides, some of which are poisonous.

There has been a lot of publicity about the dangers of poisoning from handmade pottery and many people are justifiably nervous. It would indeed be a short-sighted potter who poisoned his or her customers through carelessness or neglect. The following test has been suggested in *Tactile*, the magazine of the Canadian Guild of Potters. (This test responds to metal oxides as well as lead.)

Materials: 4 oz. white vinegar
             ⅛ teaspoonful liver of sulphur
You need two identical clear glasses.

1. Put 2 oz. vinegar in the pot to be tested and soak at room temperature for 12 hours, then put into one glass.
2. Dissolve liver of sulphur in 2 oz. of hot water.
3. Place 2 oz. fresh vinegar in the other glass.
4. Put 2 teaspoonfuls of the sulphur solution in each glass.

5. A white cloudy precipitate will form in the fresh vinegar.
6. If the test vinegar precipitate is tinged tan or brown, there are heavy metals present and the glazes deserve more accurate analysis before using on the inside of any domestic container.

If you don't want to buy ready-mixed glaze, a good starting point for making your own is: Lead bisilicate—28 parts
Cornish stone—22 parts
This will give a shiny, transparent, and colorless surface when fired to 2012° F. (1100° C.).

The following ingredients give these effects when added to a basic earthenware glaze:

Clay—up to 25% has a matting effect
Zinc oxide—up to 20% gives a matt uneven surface
Tin oxide—up to 10% acts as an opacifier
Color oxides—see chart on page 155

Stoneware glazes

Stoneware glazes are simpler than earthenware glazes because the main flux, feldspar, is a pure and trouble-free ingredient. Stoneware glazes can also be bought ready-mixed, but here are three good starting points:

Pleydell—Bouverie Ash glaze: Cone 8–9 (2300° F.–2336° F. or 1260° C.–1280° C.)
Wood ash—40 parts
Feldspar—40 parts
China or ball clay—20 parts

The effect of this glaze will vary according to the wood ash used. The properties of wood ash as a glaze were probably first discovered when flakes of burning wood fuel settled and melted on pots in the kiln. It is always worth testing any wood ash alone and you will often find ash suitable for a glaze with few, if any, additions. Ash varies greatly, and even different trees of the same species will yield ash that gives different effects. In general, slow-growing wood gives the more interesting results, but making ash glazes is always rewarding as the colors are soft and subtle.

A stoneware bottle with stopper by John J. O'Leary which has been fired with a wood-ash glaze. (Courtesy, American Crafts Council.)

111

Billington Opaque glaze: Cone 8 (2300° F. or 1260° C.)

> 24 parts feldspar
> 10 parts whiting
> 11 parts China clay
> 5 parts flint

Leach Transparent Stoneware glaze: Cone 8 (2300° F. or 1260° C.)

> 20 parts feldspar
> 5 parts China clay
> 10 parts limestone
> 15 parts quartz

To vary these glazes:

For a more matt effect: add more ball or China clay

For a shinier surface: add more whiting

For a broken color effect: add up to 10% rutile. This will also have a matting effect on the glaze.

For color: see chart of oxides on page 155

You will need two large buckets, a 60- or 80-mesh sieve and an old nailbrush. If you have a sensitive skin, wear gloves for this operation, as ash contains irritant material.

If possible, use ash burned in an indoor grate or in an incinerator that keeps the ash separate from the ground. It is much harder work to clean ash from a bonfire, but can be worth it—find out by testing a small sample as you would test a glaze. The soft, fine ash also tends to blow away from an outdoor fire, even on a calm day.

Even if it is apparently quite clean, ash needs to be washed to remove unburned material and soluble fluxes.

Having scooped up the ash as clean as you can, mix it with plenty of water and stir it well. Remove any pieces of wood, leaves, or whatever that float to the top. Then stir it vigorously again, and immediately scoop out a jugful of the liquid and pour it into the sieve. But first take the precaution of putting the sieve over a bucket. This method will allow the heavy sediment to sink to the bottom while you catch the lighter ash. Repeat the process, adding more water if necessary —plenty of water makes the sieving go faster.

When you have sieved out the ash, wait for several hours, until the ash has settled into a mass at the bottom of the bucket. Now tip off the surplus water and refill the bucket with fresh water, stirring the ash up again. Repeat this two or three times or until the water is quite clear when the ash has settled. When the last lot of water is drained away you will be left with a thick gray or black sludge. Pour or spoon it into biscuited containers (any reject bowls or vases will do for this) and leave it to dry on top of the kiln. Don't use it until it is bone dry. If any glaze ingredient is damp it won't have a true weight and will upset the glaze recipe.

It must be emphasized that I have only touched on a very involved and interesting subject, and most people will want to learn more about what they are doing. But it is possible for one to produce glazes with very little knowledge of the why and wherefore. A few more elementary remarks.

Generally speaking, the melting point of a glaze will be lowered by the number of ingredients used. If you use red clay in a glaze, remember that it is the high iron content that makes it red, and iron is a flux (a melting agent), so don't expect a matt effect. The behavior of glazes is also influenced by the composition of the body they cover. A white body will contribute to a paler glaze, and too much iron in the body may cause the glaze to bubble.

Batches of clay and glaze materials can vary considerably even if you always buy your materials from the same supplier. Always test a new batch of material. It's no good blaming the supplier, blame the geological structure of the planet and its somewhat haphazard arrangement. Perhaps this is a good place to recommend the reading of books on geology, especially interesting and instructive to the potter.

If a pot is to be used for eating, drinking, or cooking, then a glaze is necessary to give a smooth hygienic surface. Any earthenware intended to hold liquid needs a well-fitting glaze; if only on the inside of the pot, to prevent the liquid seeping through. However, the color and "feel" of the body should not always be hidden. Unglazed pots, either smooth or textured, can be very satisfying—especially if the body fires to a good color. To get a rich effect, oxides can be added to the body or painted onto leather-hard clay or biscuit.

An unglazed pot can be given a smooth polished finish by burnishing the leather-hard surface with a stone or smooth stick. A slipped surface can also be burnished, or iron oxide rubbed into the body before burnishing. Obviously, a very smooth body is most suitable for this method.

114

Making Test Glazes

If you are making test additions to a basic glaze with several ingredients, make up a large batch of basic glaze in the usual way. Pour it into a biscuited container and allow it to dry out thoroughly on top of the kiln. Weigh out small batches and work out the percentage of oxides, etc., to add. This will save the work of weighing and mixing several small amounts.

When making glaze tests keep a physical as well as a written record of what you do. The disadvantage of using pots for tests is that they can be sold or given away, and you may want to return to a line of testing after a period of time. Thrown or coiled rings of clay are good for testing glazes; they give some idea of the movement of the glaze on a perpendicular shape and can be slung together on a piece of string and take little space hung on the wall. Numbers can be painted on with oxide. Don't give up a glaze too easily, test it more than once—thicker, thinner, or over slip.

Store glazes in plastic buckets with well-fitting lids and make glazed tags with holes to tie to the bucket to show the contents. It is very important not to get pieces of powdered clay, dust, dirt, or splashes of other glazes or coloring matter in the glaze. But however careful you are, you will have to resieve the glaze occasionally. Glazes behave differently according to their composition; some dry up very easily, others go lumpy quickly, some will take a long time to settle. If you dislike insects, be warned that buckets of slurry and glaze make ideal breeding grounds, so take precautions and keep buckets very securely covered. Insecticide could be experimented with, but it might, possibly, affect the glazes. Having no objection to insects I've never tried.

Preparation for Glazing

The surface of this handsome pot has been formed by pinching the sides and textured through iron slip. It is the work of J. Sheldon Carey. (Courtesy, American Crafts Council.)

When ready to glaze you will need plenty of space—some potters use the floor, but then it must be clean. So must everything else, including you. Greasy hands will leave marks on the biscuit and glaze will not adhere to these areas. Have a bucket of water near and a sponge and towel to wipe your

115

hands on. You will make a smudgy mess if you handle a pot with glazed fingers.

Pots should also be quite clean and free from dust. If they are dusty, wipe them over with a damp sponge and give them time to dry before glazing. Slight flaws such as an over-looked smudge of slurry can be scraped off with a knife, as biscuit ware is quite soft. Don't glaze pots warm from the kiln—they will absorb too much glaze.

It is essential that no glaze remains on the foot of the pot. The glaze melts in the firing and when cooled will stick to the kiln shelf. If you want pots with a glazed base, stand them on stilts. These are triangular pieces of ceramic and can easily be knocked away after the firing, leaving only small scars where the pot rested on the points of the stilt. Stilts can be bought in different sizes, but be sure to allow for the shrinkage of any pot with a footring—it may shrink and imprison the stilt.

The neatest and quickest way to keep the base of the pot clear of glaze (and an area up to ¼″ round the base of the wall should also be kept clear, as some glazes will run down the pot) is to stand the pot briefly in melted paraffin wax. Glaze will not adhere to the waxed surface, and the wax will burn away in the firing. This wax can be bought at hardware stores. Melt the wax in an old frying pan or flat container over an electric heater or a camping stove. If you can keep the stove on low while you are working, you won't have trouble with the wax setting as it cools. Be careful with bowls that have a footring; ease the ring gently into the wax with a rotating movement, otherwise air may be trapped and cause the wax to splash over to one side. If you do get wax onto the wrong part of the pot, stand it on top of the firing kiln; there should be enough heat to melt it off. If this doesn't work, refire the pot in the biscuit kiln.

Pots with lids should be fired with the lid in position, both in the biscuit and in the glaze firing to ensure the lid fits well. All surfaces where pot and lid meet should be completely clear of glaze and care taken not to leave any thicker patches of glaze where they could run down from the lid and lock it into the pot. Wax can be applied to the galleries of lidded pots and other undippable places with a brush. Hold the pot tilted and don't overload the brush or you may drip wax all over the pot. (Brushing on melted wax in a design or

In this vase, J. Sheldon Carey has created his surface effect by using the wax-resist technique over finger impressions. (Courtesy, American Crafts Council.)

pattern is known as "wax resist." Where wax is painted directly onto the pot, the color and texture of the body will be revealed after the glazing. Wax can also be painted over one glaze which is subsequently covered by another. In this way an interesting combination of design and color can be achieved.)

Instead of using wax, you can wipe the glaze away from the bottom with a damp sponge as soon as the pot is dry enough to touch. Another method is to let the pot dry completely and brush off the surplus glaze with a toothbrush, but it is better to avoid the risk of inhaling dry glaze particles. Using the wax method saves both glaze and time.

The Process of Glazing

The easiest way to glaze pots is by dipping. Hold the pot by the footring, if it has one, or with a pair of tongs. Slip it quickly sideways into the glaze, hold it there for 1–2 seconds and then lift it smoothly out, shaking the pot as you do so. This shaking will help to distribute the glaze evenly over the surface, but watch that you don't trap a pool of glaze inside

Using tongs for dipping a mug in glaze, tilted to ensure no air is trapped. (Below left)

Glazing a small pot by holding it by the footring and lowering it into the glaze straight downward.

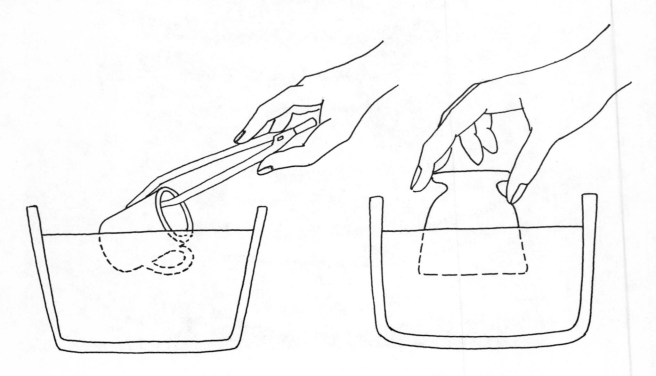

the pot. Putting the pot sideways into the glaze will prevent air from being caught inside it, which could cause an unglazed area where the trapped air prevented the glaze from coming in contact with the pot.

A small pot can be glazed inside and out by holding it by the foot, lowering it into the glaze straight downward, then lifting it and allowing the trapped air to escape, before quickly dunking it down again. This movement allows glaze to cover the inside completely—it doesn't sound easy to do and it isn't easy, but it is worth practicing.

When glazing teapots, blow gently down the spout immediately after the pot has been lifted from the glaze. This will clear the holes quickly and neatly—but be sure to check that it has done so.

The amount of water absorbed by a pot in the process of being glazed makes it heavier. Even with a small pot you need to be aware of the weight of water absorbed as, for instance, with cups and jugs. Try to lift a cup out of the glaze bucket by its handle and it may snap off, or use tongs to lift too heavy a pot and the tongs will cut into the biscuit as you increase pressure.

Larger pots are more easily glazed in two operations. First glaze the inside, using a jug to pour the glaze. There is no need to fill the pot, you can swirl the liquid round to coat the inner surface as you empty it out. Drips of glaze will probably run down the outer surface as you empty the pot. Perhaps these drips emphasize the line and will add to the appearance of the finished work? Then leave them. If, on the other hand, you feel they are ugly and clumsy, scrape them away with a knife when the glaze has set.

Leave the pot for a short time to allow the inside coat of glaze to dry. (You will see how the water is absorbed from the glaze into the biscuit, giving it a dark, damp appearance). There are various ways of glazing the outside of a pot, depending on its size, shape, and your preference. To glaze the outside, hold the pot by the footring or by the base and lower it gently into the glaze. Allow one or two seconds, then pull out gently again, shaking the pot meanwhile to avoid accumulations of glaze. Either use both hands to hold the pot, or use one hand to steady the working hand at the wrist.

If the pot is too difficult to grasp securely and you want a smooth overall surface with no variation of thickness, the best way is to lower the pot bottom first into the glaze until it is covered to the rim. To do this you will have to hold the pot from the inside, using both hands if it is a very large one. It isn't easy to push a big pot down quickly; you will meet resistance and you may need to thin the glaze. Shake the pot as you take it from the glaze.

Another method, more suitable if you don't have a big bucketful of glaze, is to stand the pot upside down on sticks over a large bowl. Fill a large jug with glaze—you will need more than you expect—and pour it rapidly and evenly over the base and round the outer surface, making sure that the whole area is coated. Or put the pot on a banding wheel inside a bowl and turn the pot on the wheel while pouring the glaze. However, this results in a lot of washing up.

With practice you can learn to support a pot from the inside with the left hand and turn it as you pour glaze from the jug with your right hand.

A wooden coat hanger makes a good substitute for sticks, and often the neck of a pot will fit inside the angle of the hanger and the rim won't be lumpy with glaze accumulating

A way of supporting a large pot for glazing the outside surface.

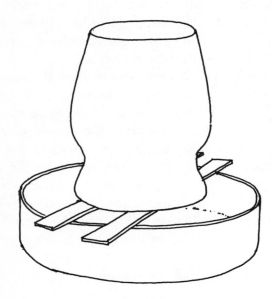

where the pot stands on the sticks. These bumps of glaze can be scraped off when dry so that the rim is evenly glazed, or it may be necessary to scrape off all the glaze from the rim and use the banding wheel to rotate the pot and brush on fresh coats. Several coats of glaze may be necessary in order to build up as thick a coat as covers the rest of the pot. Allow each coat to dry before applying the next, otherwise the glaze will lift off. You can test the thickness of a glazed surface by scratching it lightly with a finger nail.

When glazing several pieces stir the glaze frequently. With some glaze mixtures the particles settle to the bottom of the container very rapidly.

Large pieces can be glazed by dipping if you have a large enough container, strong hands, and plenty of confidence, but it is a tricky process. Try to hold the pot where finger marks can easily be camouflaged, or where they will enhance the design. The touching up of finger marks needs to be very carefully done if they are not to leave a clumsy blemish on the surface of the pot. The best way is to brush over more glaze when the pot is nearly dry, then scrape away any uneven patches with a knife when the glaze is quite dry. With small pots, the marks left by the finger tips can add to the appearance of the pot.

Glaze can also be applied with a spraying device, but this is messy to use without a special booth and an air extractor that sucks away the surplus glaze particles before you can breathe them in.

You can have endless fun with glazes, trying out various combinations of color and texture. One glaze can be poured over another, either completely covering the first coat or in such a way that the shape of the pot is emphasized. Try holding different shapes at various angles or tilting the pot as you pour the glaze over it.

For a bit of action painting, take a full brush of glaze and give it a vigorous shake over or near the pot. But first take the precaution of putting newspaper behind to catch any splashes caused by too much action.

Applying two coats of glaze is called "double dipping." The first layer of glaze must be allowed to dry before the second is applied—but not to become "powder-dry." If the second coat is applied when the pot is still wet, the glaze will not adhere to the surface of the pot because the biscuit will be saturated and unable to absorb more water. On the other hand, if the first coat is bone-dry, then the second coat of wet glaze will lift the dry coat away from the pot. The result will be glaze flaws—but then, you may like them.

A simple but most effective method of emphasizing the affinity between pot and glaze is to trace quick, simple strokes through the wet glaze with your finger tips.

A soup ladle is a good tool for pouring glazes to form patterns and spoons are also useful for dripping small amounts of glaze or oxide over the pot. With a flat-shaped bowl, glaze can be spooned in and the pot tilted or shaken so that a design is formed by the glaze following the movement of the pot.

The final step before putting a pot to dry is to make sure that no particles of glaze remain on the bottom. Small bubbles of glaze can adhere to a waxed base, and a small patch of glaze can cause a lot of trouble.

A group of small vases by Ron Burke using a combination of glazes to achieve color and texture. (Courtesy, American Crafts Council.)

The Use of Oxides for Decoration

Oxides can be painted directly on the leather-hard body or painted on the biscuit, either under or over the glaze. However, if you paint oxide under a glaze, there is a risk of particles of oxide getting into the glaze batch when you dip the pot. However, it is interesting to compare the results given by the different methods of application. A very heavy concentration of manganese oxide will give a dramatic cratered effect to any glaze applied over it.

Oxides to be used for painting should be diluted with water and stored in well-labeled screw-top jars. The amount of water to be added to an oxide depends on the strength of color you require, and this can only be decided by testing. Remember that many oxides have low melting temperatures and their addition to a glaze will make it run, so play safe when testing.

When painting oxides or painting strokes for wax resist, work with the whole arm, not just from the wrist, and use smooth, flowing strokes. Think well about every design and practice on a reject pot, so that you get the right feel of the resistance met by the brush as it moves over the surface.

Ordinary house-painting brushes are good for this work. The shape of a brush can be altered by cutting some of the hairs with scissors to give a slanting or zigzag effect.

To paint bands of color round a pot, set the pot on the banding wheel, give the wheel a good pull to set it turning and bring the brush into contact with the pot until you have completed the band or until the brush is empty. If you work the brush up and down with a jigging movement, this will give a corresponding pattern.

Glaze Defects

You will be incredibly lucky if your first firing produces flawless results. Here are some of the faults you will probably find, and ways of avoiding these conditions in the future.

Underfiring

An underfired glaze has a dry, powdery appearance and "feel." However, too thinly applied stoneware glaze can also give this result. This effect is not "wrong" in itself, and it may be just what you want. If it isn't, then the pot can be refired, with another coat of glaze if necessary. Underfired earthenware may craze with a loud "pinging" even when removed cool from the kiln, and the remedy is simply to refire to a higher temperature. However, if a stoneware glaze has any pinholing or crawling faults these will be intensified by the higher temperature, as the glaze will shrink away from these areas. If it is a special pot, then it might be worth applying another coat of glaze. Warm the pot, but not too much or the shock of immersion in the cold glaze will crack it. Thicken the glaze by removing some of the water from the top before stirring it up, and reglaze the pot, putting it immediately in a warm place. It's not easy to get the glaze to dry on the pot without it running down the sides and off the surface, but it can be done.

Crazing

This network of fine cracks can appear in a glaze some time after firing. This is not always a fault, indeed it is an old form of decoration and can add greatly to the appearance of a pot. Crazing is considered essential in pots used in the Japanese tea ceremony, otherwise the harsh sound of the spoon stirring the uncrazed pots disturbs the calm of the room.

Crazing is caused by the glaze not fitting the body correctly. In other words, the glaze needs to be slightly "larger" than the body. If it is not, then it will fracture when pot and glaze cool and contract. It can also be caused by the work being unpacked too quickly from the kiln and put into sudden contact with cold air. Even whole pots will sometimes fracture when exposed too suddenly to cold air, especially if they are badly made and of uneven thickness.

Crazing can generally be remedied by the addition of flint either to the glaze or to the body. This sounds contradictory, but flint has a different effect when it is part of the composition of a body than when it is part of a glaze. It is much simpler to add flint to a glaze, but if the addition of 6 per cent does not remedy the defect, try substituting boric oxide or zinc oxide for some of the glaze flux.

An ancient Chinese stoneware bowl from the Sung Dynasty shows the beautiful effect that can be achieved by crazing. (Courtesy, the Metropolitan Museum of Art, Rogers Fund, 1917.)

Peeling or Flaking

This is the reverse of crazing and occurs when the clay shrinks more than the glaze, causing the glaze to crack and pile up. This is more a stoneware fault and the remedy is to add more flux to the glaze.

Pinholing

Pinholes are tiny holes that appear in the raw glaze immediately after glazing. This can be caused by glazing dirty pots or by packing them in the kiln while the glaze is still damp. Always rub the holes over (unless you like a pinholed effect) when the glaze has dried. If the pinholes reappear in the firing, then add more flux to the glaze or try firing the biscuit higher.

Blistering or Cratering

This is the name for a series of volcanic craters in the glaze. This is a particularly serious flaw in tableware, as fragments of the glaze are liable to splinter off. Blistering can be caused by the firing taking place too quickly. During the firing cycle various gases escape from the glaze, and time is needed to allow these places to "heal over." Glazes will also blister over oxide too heavily applied.

Crawling

As the name implies, the glaze crawls away from some areas. This can result in a pattern all over the pot and can be most attractive. Crawling can be caused by the glaze being applied to dirty ware or to ware too damp to absorb it. It can also be the result of the glaze being too thickly applied or of the pot being placed in the kiln and fired before the glaze has had a chance to dry.

USE AND CARE OF THE KILN

You should receive instructions with the kiln for the firing cycle as well as how to dry out the brickwork before the first firing. It is usually stressed that this should not be to a high temperature; some manufacturers recommend a long period with the kiln on low and the door open, others suggest one or more very slow, low firings. If the kiln is powered by electricity, never leave it too long without firing or there is danger that the elements may become rusty or the contacts damaged by dampness. If you have no pots to fire, turn the power on low once a week for an hour or so, leaving the door open.

Kiln Furniture

Kiln furniture; i.e., kiln shelves and shelf supports can usually be bought with the kiln. Shelves should be 1" smaller than the interior of the kiln to allow for circulation of heat. Coat new shelves with a special kiln wash. This can be brushed on with a paintbrush and the shelves will need to be touched up if glaze drips down or the wash flakes off. Shelves and props should be included in the kiln's first drying out. If the kiln is a side loader, and the base shelf is placed on kiln props, check these regularly. If the shelf becomes warped, the props will soon crack under the uneven stress. To prevent shelves warping, always place any shelves used in a biscuit firing upside down—a kiln-washed surface is not necessary for biscuit. Always resist any temptation to sprinkle powdered kiln wash directly on a shelf, especially when it is in place in the kiln—little lumps can get into pots in a quite surprising way. If possible, place a shelf support to support the center of each shelf when packing the kiln. Incidentally, kiln shelves should be handled with great care. Being very high-fired, they are brittle and will break if dropped. However, broken shelves are very useful for testing small amounts of ash or clay to determine their melting point. A broken shelf can also be used as a "half shelf" (see page 132).

Cones

The temperature in the kiln is judged by the melting of cones. These are made from cone-shaped ceramic material that will melt and bend over when the stated temperature is reached. Cones are placed inside the kiln and viewed through the "spy hole." Each cone is numbered for identification. They are delicate and need to be stored carefully in a dry place—if dropped, the fracture may not be visible but the cone will fall apart in the firing. It is rare to have a faulty cone, but it can happen. For this reason, and also to have warning before you reach temperature, it is usual to place three cones of different melting temperatures, one to give warning you are approaching the temperature needed, one for the actual temperature and one for the higher temperature in case of overfiring. Special holders can be bought for cones, otherwise support them firmly in a small pad of clay. If you do this and fire the kiln before the clay has time to dry, prick the clay pad several times to allow the air to escape. Otherwise the clay may shatter when heated rapidly—and where then are the cones? Out of sight and a firing wasted.

There are three different kinds of cones on the market: seger cones, orton cones, and miniature orton cones. These three ranges have different firing temperatures, and it is easy to become confused. A list of these different cone numbers and the temperatures to which they fire is given in the Appendix, together with a color guide to temperatures.

The more sophisticated and also the more expensive way to judge kiln temperature is to fit a pyrometer. This gives a constant reading of the temperature within the kiln but is not completely reliable and most potters rely on cones. You can also buy switches called "kiln watchers" to be fitted to the kiln that will cut the current off when the required temperature is reached, but here also it is wiser to set cones and watch them yourself.

Packing for a Biscuit Firing

For earthenware, the biscuit should be fired to a temperature of 2012° F. (1100° C.). For stoneware it is only necessary to fire the biscuit to 1724° F., (940° C.) as the work will subsequently be fired higher. The higher the biscuit is fired, the less porous it becomes and the less absorbent, therefore if you should underfire the biscuit, it is well to thin the glaze slightly. If you overfire the biscuit, on the other hand, use the glazes thicker or warm the pots slightly.

Essential to packing any kiln: bone-dry pots, a calm mind, and plenty of time. For biscuit, pots can be packed inside each other, but watch it if you have used different kinds of clay—some may shrink more than others, imprisoning any pots packed inside. Pack big pieces first, in the middle if they are flat and likely to distort, and place smaller pieces round them. If stacking pots on top of each other, make sure a heavy piece does not threaten a fragile one beneath. Bowls, saucers, and plates should be packed rim to rim, provided they are of equal size. Lids should be fired in place. They will fit better if fired together, both in the biscuit and glaze firings.

When you have loaded the first shelf, check by passing a useful stick across the door or top of the kiln supports to make sure the pots are well *inside* and will not be damaged when you close the door or, in the case of a top loader, when the next shelf is placed in position. Check the cone setting with great care, using a lighted candle to see its position through the spy hole when the door is shut. Make sure the tip of the cone will not go out of sight as it melts and bends over. Never open and attempt to repack the kiln and reposition the cone once the firing has started as the warm damp air will have penetrated the cone and softened it so that it may collapse.

Biscuit Firing

The first stages of firing should take place very slowly. If no firing chart was supplied with the kiln, allow at least six hours on low with the spy hole out to allow moisture to escape. This is known, poetically, as the "water smoking period." This moisture includes what is known as "chemically combined water" which is released from the clay at a temperature of between 660° F.–930° F. (350° C.–500° C.). At this stage the clay is dehydrated and very fragile. After a temperature of 1110° F. (600° C.) has been passed the bung is put in place and the heat increased. However, the slower the firing

A packed kiln in the process of being fired.

the better, and you may prefer to leave the kiln on low all night. Turn the kiln to medium for a period of 3–4 hours before turning up to high. These remarks are only intended as a rough guide; all kilns have their own little foibles. Obviously, if the kiln has been on low for a long period the temperature will rise more steeply when it is turned up than if it had been on for only six hours. Most potters agree that firing should take place slowly and steadily. Some kilns will come to temperature on medium heat, so start watching your first firing every half hour once you have turned up the kiln.

Keep a kiln log, writing down the time taken by the firings, the behavior of the glazes, and any other remarks that occur to you. This log will give you a warning when the elements are getting tired—the firing schedule will become longer and longer. Although cones will tell you when the proper temperature has been reached, the chart in the Appendix will give a rough guide to judging the temperature by the color inside the kiln. *Always* use dark glasses when looking into red kilns—high temperatures can damage the eyes.

The kiln must be allowed to cool slowly over a period at least as long as the firing took, and preferably longer. Do not remove the bung until the inside is completely black. A sudden draught of cold air will damage the pots and also the brickwork and elements. Allow cool air to enter the kiln very gradually, first loosening the door, then opening it a chink, and so on. Discourage family and friends from bursting in and leaving an outer door open if you work in a garage or shed. The pots should be cool enough to handle easily before you unpack. But this is a counsel of perfection. Biscuit, because of its porosity, will stand reasonable changes of temperature, whereas to unpack glazed ware too soon is to invite crazing. However, unpack too hot a biscuit kiln and you shorten the life of shelves, elements, and kiln.

Packing a Glaze Firing (Earthenware or Stoneware)

Handle glazed ware gently but firmly with both hands and never pick a pot up by the rim with finger and thumb. Any glaze flaking off can be touched up. Have glaze and brush handy for this. As you pack the pots, check that the base of each piece is wiped free of glaze, since even a small particle will cause the pot to adhere to the shelf. Pots can be fired with glazed bottoms if they are packed on stilts. These are small triangular supports which can be knocked off when the fired pot is cold. If using stilts, be careful to allow for the shrinkage of the pot and be sure the pot can't trap the stilt.

Allow at least ¼″ between pieces, and be sure the pots are not too near the walls of the kiln. There is some slight expansion as the glazes melt, and the pots could stick together. Again, pack larger items first and in the middle of the kiln—also remember that bowls may sag slightly if fired high and can trap a pot packed too close underneath. Wide bowls are liable to warp when fired high, pack them in the center so that one part of the rim is not near the elements. Try to get as much work in as possible. A well-packed kiln will fire more evenly than a half-empty one. When setting up shelves in the kiln, place the props directly over the props on the shelf below so that the weight of shelves and pots is evenly supported. If possible give each shelf a central support as well, particularly if using larger shelves. Always check that the pots on the shelf below have ¼-inch clearance when the next shelf is fitted. It is, however, possible to use a "half shelf" if you have a few taller pots and want to avoid wasting kiln space. Avoid placing pots decorated or glazed with strong oxide near light-colored ones—the glaze may "travel." Of course, these random effects and so-called faults can sometimes give far more beautiful pots than were originally planned. Pack glaze tests near the mouth of the kiln where you can reach them easily—meditating about the results will help to pass the time while you wait for the kiln to cool sufficiently to finish unpacking.

When the kiln is finally packed, carry out the same precautions as for biscuit. Check that all ware is at least ¼″ *inside* the kiln and that the cone will be visible at all stages of firing.

Earthenware and Stoneware Firing

The time taken for earthenware and stoneware firing causes some controversy, but with an electric kiln it is certainly much healthier to fire it slowly, allowing 9–10 hours for earthenware glaze and 12–14 hours for stoneware.

Again, leave the spy hole open and the kiln on low for 1½–2 hours. This allows the moisture remaining in the glazes to escape before the kiln is closed and the heat turned to medium. However thoroughly the glazed ware has been dried (and it is a good idea to set pots to dry on top of the kiln as wet pots will develop serious glaze defects) there will be some moisture remaining. You can test if the air from the kiln is quite dry with a mirror or spectacles held over the spy hole (always assuming that you can then see sufficiently well to observe any signs of moisture on the glass). Remember that if the pottery is very cold, there will be condensation where the warm air of the kiln escapes through the spy hole and meets the cold air, but it is important to be sure that all damp air has been driven from the kiln before closing it completely.

You will probably need to leave the heat on medium for 6–8 hours, but this will depend on the speed at which the temperature builds up in the kiln—some kilns fire far more quickly than others, and the firing schedule must be adjusted accordingly. You will have some idea of how the firing will go from your experience with biscuit firing and certainly don't need a warning to watch it carefully! At least 20 minutes should elapse between one cone melting and the next going down, but it may be considerably longer. For the first firing, start watching ten minutes after the first cone goes down, just in case your kiln is a fast worker.

Allow the kiln to cool slowly. In other words, leave it strictly alone—no leaving an outer door open or blowing cold fans or emptying ice cubes around. Take the same precautions about opening up as for biscuit, only more so, because it is harder to resist the desire to peep.

Unpacking a Glaze Firing

Glazed pots exposed too quickly to cold air will sometimes break—especially if they are unevenly potted—and the glazes will certainly craze. They should be cool enough to handle easily before being taken from the kiln and put in a warm place. Rub the bottom over with carborundorum stone to give a smooth under surface that will not scratch the furniture.

If any pots have stuck to the kiln shelf because of the

glaze running down, they may come off without any assistance when completely cold because the pot and shelf will contract at different rates. If any work remains obstinately stuck, try tapping it off with a hammer and chisel. But first decide which matters more to you, the shelf or the pot, and attack the one that means least. Lids are sometimes difficult to remove, but a sharp tap all round the outer edge of the pot with the handle of a screwdriver, or some other tool, will usually solve this problem. If small bits of glaze or shelf are stuck to the base of the pot, they can be ground off with an electric drill and grinding attachment.

Now, when the excitement of the firing has died down, is a good time to check over those precious shelves and repaint them with kiln wash if necessary. If odd pieces of pot or drips of glaze are stuck to the shelf, chip them off with a hammer and cold chisel before repainting the shelf.

Once-fired Ware

The point of having two firings is to make glazing easier. Applying glaze to raw ware is a tricky business and the advantage of saving time and money in once-fired ware is generally off-set by a higher failure rate.

However, for unglazed pots and slip-glazed stoneware (see page 102) a single firing saves time and trouble. Slip glaze is applied when the pots are leather-hard and, being composed entirely of clay, will adhere to the pot without cracking. The firing proceeds as for biscuit, but is taken straight up to stoneware temperature.

Salt-glazed Stoneware

Salt glazing is a very different technique from ordinary glazing and can only be carried out in a kiln with a through draft. The ware is fired only once, and at a temperature of about 2012° F. (1100° C.) common salt is dropped or pushed into the kiln through the spy hole. The salt immediately vaporizes and coats the surface of the pots. The adding of salt

An 18″ stoneware vase by Conway Pierson that has been slip glazed. (Photo by Ann Perkoff. Courtesy, American Crafts Council.)

Salt-glazed pot by Michelle Schloessink-Paul. (Photo by Michael Hentges.)

An unusual piece of salt-glazed stoneware by Don Reitz. (Courtesy, American Crafts Council.) (Right)

137

A set of reduction-fired bowls by Vally Possony. (Photo by Claire Flanders.)

is repeated two or three times between 2012° F. (1100° C.) and 2192° F.–2282° F. (1200° C.–1250° C.). Not only does the vapor coat the surfaces of the pots, it coats the kiln interior as well. Indeed, several firings are needed before the walls of the kiln begin to "give back" the glaze to the pots, as the new bricks will absorb the glaze in the first firings. The color of the glaze will be influenced by the color of the body, but pots already glazed or slipped can be fired in a salt kiln and many different colors and textures obtained.

This is an exciting technique, but not for the beginner working in a small way. A high failure rate in the early stages of learning the technique is almost inevitable. Also, the vapor escapes from the kiln in the form of hydrochloric acid, and this is a corrosive substance. Salt glazing should never be attempted in an electric kiln.

Reduction Firing

Reduction is the name given to the process of introducing combustible material such as moth balls or carbon into the kiln at about 2012° F. (1100° C.). The chemical energy of this sudden combustion is such that it draws out all the oxygen in body, glaze, and oxides to consume the material. This has the effect of imparting very delicate colors to the glazes. If iron is present in the body in small amounts, it will break through the glaze, giving it a speckled texture.

Unfortunately, reduction firing is not recommended for electric kilns as all this activity seriously affects the elements.

Getting to Know the Kiln

If your kiln has a large spy hole that has to be taken out to look at the cones, you may find the area round it to be slightly cooler than the rest of the kiln. It is a good idea to place sets of cones in different parts of the chamber at different levels and thus learn what temperatures are reached where.

Uneven firing can sometimes be remedied with a longer soaking period. However, if the kiln temperature is persistently low in one part of the kiln, then you must adapt yourself and pack it accordingly with glazes that mature at the lower temperature in the cooler place.

"Flashing" is a shiny patch of glaze, melted by a local higher temperature. This takes place in some kilns on that part of the pot placed nearest the element, where the heat is highest. This fault can often be overcome by turning the heat to medium when the cone starts to bend (or on the bending of the previous cone) and "soaking" on medium temperature for up to an hour. The temperature in the elements will be raised more slowly and have time to penetrate the kiln. This soaking is generally considered good for glazes, particularly earthenware, with its shorter firing schedule, as it allows time for the smoothing over of any blisters or craters caused by gas escaping from the glaze in the earlier stages of firing. Many potters soak as a matter of course. Alternatively, try packing the pots farther from the elements.

Care of the Kiln

Keep an eye out for loose pieces of brickwork in the roof and sides of the kiln. This should not be necessary with a new kiln, but time creeps up on one, and the bricks can easily be chipped with the edge of a shelf when packing or unpacking. Check the elements frequently to make sure no small pieces of clay or glaze have adhered to them. If you do have a blowout through packing a pot too thick or damp, be particularly careful that no pieces of clay have become wedged in the element coils. Vacuum the kiln carefully and never put another thick or damp pot in again. Thick pieces may survive if fired very slowly, but blowouts sometimes occur if air is trapped in the clay. This can happen even in a thin pot. A small piece of stone or plaster in the clay can also cause a blowout.

Another thing that can go wrong is that a cone can melt over the edge of the shelf and drip over an element—and that's one element the fewer. This can be avoided by setting the cone where, if it should melt, it will do so onto the shelf.

Don't attempt to run the kiln an element short, you won't reach the correct temperature. Many kilns are wired so that they do not work at all if an element breaks, and this may well be the way you discover the damage: The temperature in the kiln will go down instead of rising. On the other hand, if the kiln is wired on separate circuits, power will still be going through, but not enough to raise the temperature at the normal rate. If the firing seems inordinately long, turn off the power and wait until the next day to find out the worst. It is very unlikely that the firing will be ruined, only in the early stage of biscuit would the pots be too fragile to remove from the kiln intact. If the element were *that* weak, you would surely have noticed.

Many potters prefer to change an element or set of elements before trouble begins—it is easy to see when the danger point is near—the wiring becomes uneven and bunchy and the wire looks white and brittle. Sometimes dark spots appear. This sounds like a disease, but if you fire consistently to a high temperature, you must expect a certain element mortality and be prepared for the expense. On the other hand, if you fire only to earthenware temperature and treat the kiln with respect, the elements may last many years.

However, changing elements is not a difficult job—not much more complicated than changing the element of an electric heater. You merely disconnect the connections, extract the old element and replace it with the new, then screw everything up again. Be sure screws are really firm. A loose connection will cause "arcing." Need I say: always disconnect the power before you do anything in the works? Trouble will come if the element burned out at high temperature and fused into the brickwork. Chipping out the precious brickwork to remove all the metal can be an unpleasant job. It's best to ease out the damaged part of the brick with a screwdriver rather than use a hammer and chisel. The gentler you are with the soft brickwork the better. Any holes in the brick can be filled in with special kiln cement.

You can see the advantages of changing the elements *before* strictly necessary and resisting the temptation to get a little more work from them. Don't forget to vacuum clean the kiln to remove any loose pieces and to brush the element grooves clear with a clean paintbrush before fitting the new elements.

SETTING UP A WORKROOM

So much has been written about ergonomics and work flow that it is probably unnecessary to make any remarks about avoiding endless wanderings from clay to wheel and from pot to kiln. Unfortunately, anyone making do with limited facilities can't always put equipment in the most efficient place.

Ideally, you need a large area, and the work flow should be: stored clay, pugmill,* wedging surface, wheel, space for pots, kick wheel for turning, plenty of space to dry pots, large area for assembly, shelves for drying, storage for glaze ingredients, place for mixing and applying glazes with water laid on, shelf for drying glazed ware, kiln, space for unpacking kiln, and, finally, shelves on which to put your finished work. This ideal is beyond most of us—certainly at the start of a potting life. But one can make the best use of limited possibilities, and maybe a bit of advice on essentials will cut out some of the trial and error.

Some form of heating for the pottery or place where you work is essential in winter. Without hot air, you may find yourself in the sad state of having no dry pots to fill the kiln until you can fire the kiln to dry the pots. Carrying work about and putting it near the radiators in the house is obviously risky in the average home, even if the rest of the family approves. I don't recommend drying pots in the oven; unless you have the heat on very low and the door open the pots will probably shatter.

Good lighting is very important; work as near to a window as possible, or under a light. As to artificial lighting, strip lighting gives a good shadow-free area, but shadows have their place in this world of shape and form, and will give you ideas. Try and fix a movable lamp on a long wire. A mirror will make an extra eye for you, especially if propped up near the wheel.

Having a water connection in your workroom is a great advantage, but who would forego the joys of potting because of the extra work of carrying a bucket of water now and then? Maybe you can run a hose from a tap in the house. Fittings

* This is a machine for mixing clay and is a most labor-saving piece of equipment, but beyond the reach of most beginners as it is expensive.

can be bought to turn a hose on and off like a tap. If you are lucky enough to have a washable floor in the workroom, the best way to clean up is to use a hose to flood the place and brush water, dirt, and all out the door. Unfortunately, this is not a practical suggestion if you live in an urban community.

Temporary shelves can be made with planks supported by stacked bricks on each end. An old tea wagon is a most useful thing to have. Even if distance is not a consideration, it is an advantage to have the area of mobile work space that this will provide.

You will need a really firm table for wedging. It is worth taking the trouble to get this exactly the right height to work at without unnecessary fatigue. The most efficient surface is achieved by building a structure of bricks cemented to the floor, but most of us make do with a strong, secondhand table. If your table has an uneven or splintered top, nail planks or a sheet of hard board over it. Then nail a layer of sacking or strong material over the area you will use for wedging. A thick slab of marble gives an excellent wedging surface, but marble is not easy to come by—don't be misled into thinking that slate will do just as well as the surface slowly splinters away into the clay when it is used in this way.

When arranging equipment, remember that particles of clay can splash a long way, both from wedging and from the wheel. Try to make sure that they will land where they will do no harm, or you may find unexpected decoration on fresh pots or ruined glaze surfaces on those awaiting firing.

One is not always free to work on pots when they are just dry enough, and they need to be kept in a state of suspended dampness until you have time to finish them. A large tin will make a very small damp cupboard, or pots can be placed, bat and all, inside a polythene bag. One of the advantages of working at home is that you can keep an eye on things, perhaps popping in to stick on a handle between one chore and another. But never do this sort of thing with pans on the stove, these jobs always take longer than you expect. A proper damp cupboard is very good to have, one cannot always speed the parting guest because the saucers need turning. You can buy a ready-made damp cupboard, but they are expensive and an old refrigerator or a completely airtight cupboard may be the answer. Few cupboards are airtight, but a plaster-of-paris block can be made (see page 146) and soaked in water. Left in the cupboard it will maintain the moisture content of the air. If this is still not damp enough, you can make a block of plaster of paris with a deep indentation at one end, which can be filled with water. A curtain can be fixed on the shelf above and the end of the curtain trail in the water. This will give a very damp atmosphere, but will probably breed damp (or dry) rot in the cupboard. Life is never perfect.

I've already advised that the more clay you can store, and the longer you can store it, the better. If you have storage bins, remove the clay from its polythene bag—the moisture tends to draw out of the clay and condense on the inside of the bag. A sheet of polythene over the top of the bin under the lid prevents the clay drying out. With a badly fitting bin lid, it may be necessary to put a damp towel over the clay under the polythene. This is also a good way to dampen down a stiff lump of clay.

Ash should also be stored dry and covered while waiting to be washed, and after being washed and dried it should be kept in a covered container.

I've said so often "label this" and "label that," but labels are very much a risk in a pottery. Ordinary paper labels won't last long, but the plastic kind that are punched out with a tool and can be stuck on will stand the life.

Leather-hard clay turnings can be picked up in handfuls (provided there are no hard bits among them), dipped quickly in slurry or water and put straight back in the clay-for-wedging bin. Up to a point, clay improves with being worked, rejected, and reclaimed, but if used too frequently will become "tired"—too weary to work at all. This is not the same as what happens when clay is thrown too long. It should then be mixed with fresh clay and left awhile.

To dry out clay from the slurry bin, use plaster-of-paris blocks, biscuit pots, or old kiln shelves. Whatever you use to contain the clay, the mass will dry out more rapidly if the container is supported on props—bricks or kiln props—so that the air can circulate all around.

Water containing clay should never be poured light-heartedly down the drains, it will rapidly block them up. Schools with potteries have a clay trap fitted to prevent this, but it's better to avoid even washing your hands under the house taps. If you have a deep slurry bin with plenty of water always on top you can clean hands and tools from clay in this. Remember if you are working in a garage, clay and car grease make a particularly fierce combination from the point of view of a drain. It isn't really necessary to risk clogging the drains. Slurry can be poured back into the slurry bin; any water containing glaze can go into a bucket for combination glaze.

If you keep all water from washing the glaze from the bottoms of pots, or from the pots themselves, in a separate bucket, you'll be surprised how soon you have a bucket of combination glaze. And combination glazes are often the best of all, being unrepeatable. Sieve the contents of the bucket before testing it.

The best way to wash glaze completely from a badly glazed piece of biscuitware is to soak the whole pot in water for a few minutes. The glaze will then wipe off easily. But leaving the pot in the water too long will soften it and make it more fragile to handle. The pot will take some time to dry before you can reglaze it.

You can save trouble by keeping a stick or whisk in each glaze bucket to stir between dippings. For the first mixing hands are more efficient. But don't try to save time by leaving paintbrushes in pots of oxide and water mixture. You won't waste time washing brushes, but you won't keep the brushes for long. The oxide will "eat through" the metal stock of the brush.

Wheels and kilns are pretty straightforward pieces of equipment, but if anything should go wrong you may have to use guile to get a repair man to come. The word "pottery" has been known to alarm mechanics with no previous experience of the trade; but a good electrician can cope with a kiln, and a man used to repairing garden machinery can cope with a wheel. The phrase: "A small repair job, but it's hard to explain" should be enough. Once on the premises you will easily be able to persuade them to look at the damage, and maybe even make a convert or a customer.

Finally do remember that some of your materials will be poisonous and that those that aren't actually poisonous can't be very good for you either. So avoid the risk of swallowing anything by not taking snacks of food to the pottery and avoid inhaling any dust when you mix glazes—silica is very bad for the lungs and all clay and glazes contain a lot of silica.

Plaster of paris can be bought from potters' merchants. It needs to be used quickly as it deteriorates with time, and stale plaster will take a long time to set; indeed it may not set at all.

Be careful when using this material. If you can, work well away from your usual working area and clean up carefully afterwards. Even a small piece of plaster in a pot will attract moisture from the atmosphere which will, in time, crack the pot or cause a piece to fall out. This can happen at any stage, even after stoneware firing.

Twelve pounds of plaster will make a medium-sized block suitable for drying out clay, but experiment with mixing up a small amount first to get used to handling this rather self-willed material.

Use a plastic bowl to make the block in. The plaster can be mixed straight into it and the block will turn out easily when it has set.

To mix the plaster you will need one pint of water to each 24 ounces of plaster used. Put the water in the bowl first, then sprinkle in the plaster by hand. Shake the bowl occasionally to release any air trapped in the mixture during the process, but add the plaster as rapidly as possible. Then leave the mixture a minute before stirring it thoroughly. When it is completely mixed, leave it to set. If you have used too much water, or the plaster is a little stale, you will be able to pour off the surplus water, which will remain at the top as the plaster sets.

Never pour any plaster down the drain, it will block it very efficiently.

RAKU FIRING FOR FUN

Raku ware is traditionally used for the tea ceremony in Japan, but more and more Western potters are taking up the challenge of the technique. The ware is made of a thick, porous body which will stand up to the stress of rapid firing and even more rapid cooling. The pots are put into a red-hot kiln and taken out again at about 1571° F. (855° C.) when the glaze has melted. These factors, plus the fact that a temporary kiln can easily be built in the open air make a raku firing an ideal occasion for a party, to which you can invite those of your friends who think you're crazy, as well as those who know you aren't. If they can resist the invitation to decorate their own pot, if the sight of clay turned to solid substance before their eyes, and the magic of powdered glaze melting and hardening as it cools does not convert them—well, don't ask them next time. But few people are too young, too old, or too blasé to enjoy a raku firing.

Of course, you do need a yard—and space to avoid a fire hazard. You also need asbestos gloves and long-handled tongs, bricks for the kiln and a bit of courage to start you off. Do have a test firing first—raku parties that drag on for hours and hours over a black kiln are apt to lose their zing. A practice raku should prevent this happening. Building the kiln is a very simple matter. Ideally, use bricks that will stand a high temperature—the nearest brickyard can advise you.

The container to hold the pots and keep them from being lost or spoiled by the fire is called a "saggar" and should be made of the same clay body as the pots (see page 149).

To build the kiln: First place the saggar on bricks on level ground, with the bricks projecting in front to support a "door." Allow at least a foot all round the saggar to contain the fire and lay the bricks in a rough circle around this. Leave a gap 1" –2" between each brick, for ventilation and lay the second row of bricks over the gaps left in the first layer. This also makes the structure firmer. Leave a gap in the front of the kiln to allow access to the saggar in the second and third courses, then build over this gap so that the kiln forms a complete circle. You will need at least six courses of bricks, it is better not to build the fire up to the top of the kiln. The top of the kiln is left open.

Raku Pots

A good body for raku: 1 part stoneware clay
1 part fire clay
1 part grog

Some red clay can be substituted for the stoneware clay to give a rich color to the body.

Pots for raku are generally pinched or coiled. The body is

A raku kiln being fired.

easy to throw with, but don't try this if you have a sensitive skin; it is very gritty.

Biscuit firing in a raku kiln is a bit tricky and is better carried out in a conventional kiln. If you want your guests to have the pleasure of making their own pots as well as decorating them and watching them fired, you will have to have two parties—one well before the firing, to give time to get the pots biscuited. Pots need to be of a shape that can easily be picked up in the tongs—someone once made a miniature bath, but it was very difficult to lift out of the saggar.

Making a Saggar

Saggars can either be coiled or slabbed, depending on which technique you prefer. The slabs or coils should be 1" thick and any joins strongly made. The structure will have to stand a lot of stress, not only of heat but also of weight, with coke over and around it. The simplest form to make is in the shape of an oblong box, open at the front. A special slab can be made to serve as a door, or an old kiln shelf will serve for this. A couple of "pillars" to support the roof will strengthen the structure—but every saggar we have used has cracked. These cracks have never caused the saggar to collapse or hindered the firing of the pots, but they have caused some

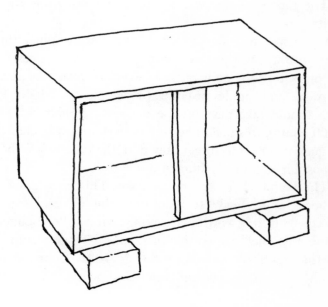

A simple slabbed saggar for raku firing.

149

alarm when seen through the fire at the beginning of the evening.

Allow the saggar to dry very slowly, and fire it to biscuit temperature. We have tried firing a saggar to stoneware temperature, but it cracked even more alarmingly than the one only biscuited. However, they both survived to the end of each day's firings.

Raku Glazes

The process of mixing and applying glazes for raku is exactly the same as for earthenware and stoneware. A basic raku glaze is composed mainly of a low-firing frit:

> 82.5 parts lead frit
> 17.5 parts ball clay

However, if you are having a party with food and children, then you would be wiser to avoid the use of lead altogether and use an alkaline frit:

> 85 parts alkaline frit
> 15 parts whiting
> 10 parts ball clay.

Tin oxide can be used as an opacifier.

Oxides can be added as coloring agents, either in the body of the glaze or painted on. Or both.

The glazing of the pots can be carried out while the kiln is heating.

Pots can either be dipped or the glaze applied thickly with a brush. Painting their pots will give your guests very great pleasure. Provide a table to work at, plenty of brushes and oxides, and candles or lamps to give plenty of light. Raku parties should take place in the darkness, or half the fun is lost. Of course, this means getting everything ready before the light goes; it is easy to forget how dark the dark is, and how it is impossible to find anything in it.

The best fuel for the fire is coke. This gives good heat and burns at a steady temperature. Not all coal suppliers stock coke, but it is worth persevering as it can be obtained. If you use this fuel, remember that coke gives off fumes, so build the mouth of the kiln on the side away from the wind. Start the fire with paper and wood and a little coke or coal.

Add more fuel as it gets going until the kiln is full. The kiln should come to temperature within two or three hours, but this will depend on the site of your kiln and on the weather. Keep the fire well stoked, even when the temperature is high enough, so that you can keep firing pots without having to wait while the fire gets up again.

You can also fire raku using wood for fuel, but be sure to have a large supply at hand. You will need to feed the fire continually, as wood burns rapidly.

While the fire is getting hot set the glazed pots to dry on the top bricks of the kiln.

When the space inside the saggar is colored by the fire it is time to put the pots in. Wear asbestos gloves (or strong gloves wrung out in water) and use the tongs to pick the pots up one by one and put them in the saggar. Don't get bothered if they fall over or touch each other; you will remove them when the glaze is liquid and they won't stick together. Use the tongs to prop the door up against the saggar, and then you have to wait.

The actual firing will probably take 10–20 minutes, but this, again, will depend on wind and weather conditions. Use the tongs to tilt the door and look inside the saggar. You will see the pots shining when the glaze melts. Give them a few more minutes for luck, then lift away the door and pick the first pot out with the tongs.

The most dramatic form of cooling a raku pot is to plunge it immediately into a bucket of water. The water will bubble and give off steam from the heat of the pot, and you then lift the pot out and set it down to cool.

When the glowing red pot is taken from the kiln and set on the ground, the shine of the glaze will gradually appear as it cools. However, the least dramatic form of cooling raku pots often has the most exciting results. Dip the red-hot pot immediately in a container full of sawdust or burned leaves and cover it over. The burning of this material will give a primitive form of reduction, but the pot must then be plunged in cold water to "set" the reduced glaze.

Do remember that such low-fired ware is not safe to eat or drink from and that food and drink should be kept well away from glaze-stained fingers and glaze containers. (We're probably the only family to have had red lead in the dish-washer—but that's another story.)

Raku pot by Harry Horlock Stringer. (Right)

Raku pot by Harry Horlock Stringer. Wax-resist areas in the glaze are blackened when the pot is reduced.

Raku tea bowl made by John Chalke. Decorated by Kenji Funaki for the tea ceremony. (Taggs Yard, 1969.)

APPENDIX

Coloring Oxides

Cobalt oxide:	¼–1%	gives pale–strong blue
Iron oxide:	1%–10%	gives yellow–brown
Copper oxide:	2–5%	gives light–dark green
Manganese oxide:	2–6%	gives purple–brown

Copper+cobalt=blue–green
Copper+Manganese=brown, black
Copper+rutile=warm textured green

Iron+cobalt=gray–blue
Iron+copper=warm green–black
Iron+manganese=brown

Manganese+cobalt=blue–purple
Manganese+rutile=brown

Cobalt+rutile=textured blue

Many more combinations of color can be obtained. When two or more oxides are used in a glaze, the amounts of each should be reduced slightly, otherwise the color will be very dark.

List of Cones, Temperatures, and Color Guide

(This is not the complete range)

SEGER CONES	ORTON CONES	MINIATURE ORTON CONES	TEMPERATURE °F.	TEMPERATURE °C.	COLOR
				600	Begins to show cherry-red
010		012	1652	900	
	010		1661	905	
09		010	1688	920	
	09		1706	930	
08		09	1724	940	
	08		1742	950	
07			1760	960	
		08	1801	983	
06			1796	980	
	07		1814	990	

SEGER CONES	ORTON CONES	MINIATURE ORTON CONES	TEMPERATURE °F.	°C.	COLOR
05			1832	1000	Bright cherry-red
		07	1846	1008	
	06		1859	1015	
04			1868	1020	
		06	1873	1023	
03	05		1904	1040	
02	04		1940	1060	Redness starts to turn orange
		05	1944	1062	
01			1976	1080	
		04	2008	1098	
1			2012	1100	
		03	2068	1131	
	03		2039	1115	
2			2048	1120	
	02		2057	1125	
3			2084	1140	
	01		2093	1145	
		02	2098	1148	
4	1		2120	1160	Bright, light orange
	2		2129	1165	
	3		2138	1170	
		01	2152	1178	
5		1 & 2	2154	1179	
	4		2174	1190	
		3	2185	1196	
6			2192	1200	
		4	2208	1209	Orange starts turning to white
	5		2201	1205	
		5	2230	1221	
7	6		2246	1230	
8	7		2282	1250	
		6	2291	1255	
	8		2300	1260	
		7	2307	1264	
9			2336	1280	
	9		2345	1285	White
10		8	2372	1300	
	10		2381	1305	
		9	2403	1317	

GLOSSARY

Albany Slip	Used as a slip or glaze ingredient.
Atmosphere Hard	Clay dried out of all non-chemically combined water and ready for firing.
Ball Clay	A very plastic clay used in bodies and glazes.
Banding Wheel or Whirler	Small wheel turned by direct action of the hand, used for coiling and decorating pots.
Barnard Clay	A slip or a glaze ingredient, gives shades of brown.
Bats	Circular discs made of plywood, hard board, or plaster. For throwing on the wheel or placing pots on to dry.
Beating	Hitting a pot with a paddle or stick to shape it.
Biscuit or Bisque	The first firing—low so that the pot will be porous and "take" the glaze. Also used to describe pots that have been biscuit fired.
Blistering or Cratering:	A glaze fault when craters or blisters form.
Bloating	Blisters in the body caused by overfiring.
Body	A clay, or mixture of clays, used to make pots.
Calcining	Pre-firing to red heat to make materials easier to grind.
Carbonates	Coloring materials for glazes. They are more stable than oxides as the base is combined with carbon as well as oxygen.
Celadon	A particular ware with a pale green, reduced, stoneware glaze. Also used to describe the type of glaze.
Centering	Getting the clay exactly in the center of the wheelhead when throwing or trimming.
Chamotte	Calcined clay used as grog in coarse bodies to give added strength and a rough texture. Used in refactory bodies.
Chattering	A broken pattern resulting from trimming with a blunt tool.
China Clay	Pure white clay used in bodies and in glazes as a matting agent.
Chuck	Support to hold a pot on the wheel for trimming. A chuck can be either a fired pot, a biscuited or a leather-hard shape.
Cobalt Oxide	Blue coloring for glazes.
Coiling	Forming a pot by building up coils of clay.
Collaring	Narrowing the neck of a pot on the wheel.
Cones	Used to tell temperature in the kiln. Small cone-shaped pieces of ceramic numbered to the temperature at which they will melt.
Coning	On the wheel, bringing the clay up to a cone shape to mix the clay properly before forming the pot.

Copper Oxide	Coloring giving green coloring. Under reduction, it gives a red effect.
Crawling	A glaze fault: The glaze leaves bald patches on the pot.
Crazing	A network of fine hair cracks in the surface of a glaze.
Dolomite	Glaze ingredient, giving a matt effect in stoneware.
Double Dipping	Dipping a pot in two different glazes.
Dunting	Pots cracking as a result of too-rapid cooling.
Earthenware	Pots fired between 1904° F.–2120° F. (1040° C.–1160° C.).
Elements	Coiled wires that heat electric kilns.
Engobe	Slip for coarse clays.
Feathering	Slip decoration where lines of slip are drawn across to give a feathered effect.
Feldspar	Main stoneware glaze ingredient, also used in bodies. Raises firing temperature of a body.
Flashing	A shiny area on a glazed pot caused by faulty firing.
Flint	Glaze and body ingredient. Will improve glaze fit as it has a high coefficient of expansion.
Flux	A melting agent.
Gallery	Indented rim to support a lid.
Glaze	Composed mainly of silica, a surface covering for the pot, to fulfill various functions, beauty, color, tactile pleasure, ease of cleaning, etc.
Grog	Previously fired clay, ground down. Used to make body stronger and more malleable.
Iron Oxide	Gives yellow to brown in glazes, red in bodies.
Kiln Furniture	Painted on shelves and supports, prevents pots adhering to the shelves or the supports sticking to the shelves.
Kiln Wash	Shelves and supports used in the kiln.
Kneading	Process of mixing clay for throwing.
Knuckling or Pulling Up	Thinning the wall of a thrown pot.
Marbling	Different colored slips flowing together. Also a technique of using different colored clays.
Modeling	Forming a clay figure with the hands.
Nepheline Syenite	A glaze material.
Oxides	Coloring materials for glazes, a combination of metal and oxygen.
Peeling	A glaze fault, similar to crawling.
Pinch Pots	Small pots, pinched with the fingers.
Pinholing	A glaze fault, tiny holes in the surface.
Porcelain	Fine, white ware fired above 2372° F. (1300° C.).
Powder Dry	Glaze completely dry, it will powder off when touched.
Pugmill	A clay mixing machine.

Pulling	Forming handles by pulling and squeezing clay into shape.
Pyrometer	Used for measuring the temperature while the kiln is firing.
Raku	Low-fired pots fired and cooled rapidly.
Reduction Firing	High firing in which combustible material is introduced to the kiln giving special effects to the pots. The burning of the material draws oxygen from the glaze and body.
Refactory Materials	Materials also to stand high temperatures such as those used in kiln building, etc.
Rutile	Glaze ingredient, giving broken and mottled effects.
Saggar	Container for pots when firing to glaze. For raku, or in a large kiln instead of shelves and to protect pots from direct flames when gas or wood is used as fuel.
Salt Glazing	A high firing process, where salt is introduced to the kiln and vaporizes, coating the pots.
Sgraffito	Method of decoration, scratching through a layer of slip or glaze to show color beneath.
Short Clay	Clay insufficiently plastic to work easily.
Slabbing	Assembling pots from slabs of clay.
Silica	Basic component of clays and glazes.
Sintering	Glaze beginning to melt during the course of the firing.
Slip	A thin mixture of clay and water. Can be colored for decorative use.
Slip Glaze	Clay with a sufficiently low melting point to use as a glaze.
Slurry	Thick mixture of clay and water, or used to describe reclaimed clay settling in the slurry bin.
Smooth Clay	Clay which is smooth and plastic.
Soaking	Slowing the firing by turning the heat down. This allows the heat to circulate from the elements and gives glazes more time to mature.
Soft Glaze	Low-fired glaze
Stoneware	High-fired ware, 2282° F.–2372° F. (1250° C.–1300° C.).
Throwing	Forming pots on the rotating wheel.
Tin Oxide	Glaze ingredient used as an opacifier in earthenware (rendering the glaze opaque).
Under Firing	When the glaze does not reach the temperature needed to melt it sufficiently.
Water-smoking Period	The kiln is left with the spy hole out or the door or lid slightly open to allow moisture to escape at the beginning of the firing cycle.
Wax Resist	Painting on wax for special glaze effects.
Wedging	Method of mixing and de-airing clay.
Whiting	Glaze ingredient—lowers melting point of glazes.
Wood Ash	Used as a glaze or a glaze component.

SUPPLIERS AND BIBLIOGRAPHY

Wheels and Kilns

A. D. Alpine, Inc., 353 Coral Circle, El Segundo, Calif. 90245.

Robert Brent, Potters Wheels, 1101 Cedar Street, Santa Monica, Calif. 90405.

L & L Kilns, Box 348, 144 Conchester Road, Twin Oaks, Pa. 19104.

Paragon Industries, Inc., Dept. CM, Box 10133, Dallas, Tex. 75207. (Kilns)

Shimpo-West, P. O. Box 2315, La Puente, Calif. 91746. (Wheels)

Unique Kilns, HED Industries, Inc., Box 176, Pennington, N.J. 08534.

Westby Kilns, Dept. CM, 408 72nd Street, NE, Seattle, Wash. 98115.

Clays, Glazes, and Tools

Minnesota Clay Co., 2410 38th Street, Minneapolis, Minn. 55406.

Ohio Ceramic Supply, Inc., Box 630, Kent, Ohio 44340.

Standard Ceramic Co., Box 435, Pittsburgh, Pa. 15205.

Bibliography and Further Reading

Behrens, Richard, *Glaze Projects*, (A Ceramics Monthly Handbook), Prof. Publications, Inc.

Billington, Dora, *The Technique of Pottery*, B. T. Batford, Ltd., London.

Eley, Vincent, *A Monk at the Potters Wheel*, Edmund Ward.

Fieldhouse, Murray, *Pottery*, Foyles Handbook.

Fraser, H. and Ceram, L., *Kilns and Kilns Firing*, Pitman Publishing Corp., New York.

Green, David, *Understanding Pottery Glazes*, Faber and Faber, Ltd., London.

———— *Pottery Materials and Techniques*, Fred A. Praeger, New York.

Leach, Bernard, *A Potter in Japan*, Faber and Faber, Ltd., London.

———— *A Potter's Book*, Faber and Faber, Ltd., London.

Norton, F. H., *Elements of Ceramics*, Addison-Wesley Publishing Co., Inc., Reading, Mass.

Rhodes, David, *Clay and Glazes for the Potter*, Pitman Publishing Corp., New York.

———— *Stoneware and Porcelain*, Pitman Publishing Corp., New York.

Sanders, Herbert H., *The World of Japanese Ceramics*, Kodanska Int., Ltd.

Soldner, Paul, *Kiln Construction*, American Craftsmen's Council, 1965.